Denham Described

A History of Denham Golf Club
1910 - 1992

J.C. Hibbert, a founder member
and our first captain

Denham Described

A History of Denham Golf Club
1910 - 1992

by

Michael Melford

with contributions and research by

Bob Fenning

Grant Books, Worcestershire
1992

ISBN 0 907186 23 8

Typeset in Baskerville by
Bigwood and Staple Limited

Published for Denham Golf Club

by

Grant **Hobbs**

Grant Books
Victoria Square, Droitwich,
Worcestershire WR9 8DE

Denham Described

The Sponsors

The Hon. Sir Scott Baker
Sir Hugh Bidwell
Kingsley Borrett
Ashley Brewer
Geoffrey & Shirley Brewer
Richard Cawdron
Donald & Rosie Chilvers
Carl Chronander
Wallace & Catherine Clapperton
Denis Compton
John & Adrienne Corbishley
Jerry Davis, California, USA
Robert Farr
Andrew Fenning
Patricia Ferguson
Patricia Gethin
Gill & Sandy Gibbins
John & Gillie Gordon
Robin Griffiths,
    Southampton, Hampshire
Ian Groom
Nigel Hague
John Henderson
Dr Donald Holmes,
    Ringwood, Hampshire
Louis Hughes
Diana Hunter, Barbara Hicks &
    Jacqueline Nalder
Kenneth Janke,
    Bloomfield Hills, Michigan, USA
David Jones
Peter Johnsen
Hugh & Sue Lang
David Loveridge
Donald, Kate & Michael MacKeith
Angus McCallum
Mary & Sandy McIntosh
The Marshall Family
Meg Moeran
Mal Morgan
Jim Murphy-O'Connor
Douglas Neave
Geoffrey Owen & Family
John, Sarah & Harry Owen

Jeffrey & Beryl Payne
Malcolm Pearson,
    Todenham, Gloucestershire
Prestwick Golf Club
R.S. Pringle, Old Troon
    Sporting Antiques, Troon
Chris Radbone
Derek Redfern
Frank F. Reia, Ontario, Canada
Hamish & Carol Ritchie
Martin Ritchie
Mark & Joan Russell
John & Jenny Sanders
David & Ian Sayers
Peter & Cathee Sedgwick
John Sheridan
David Simons
Heather & Bill Sloley
Billy Steel
Donald Steel
Philip & Elizabeth Stephens
John & Biddy Stevenson
Derek Stewart
Gilmour Thom
Gwen & Malcolm Thomas
Kerry Thomas
Philip A. Truett,
    Croydon, Surrey
John & Sorrel Trumper
Jonathan Turner
Dr Jan Vandamme, Ronse, Belgium
Reg Vowels
Kim & Fiona Walker
Robert & Hilary Walker
The Walkinshaw Family
Brian & Susie Webb
Keith Williams,
    Hawkstone Park, Shropshire
Caroline Wilson
Daniel Wilson
John Wright
James & Jill Yarrow
Charles M. Yaws,
    Prairie Village, Kansas, USA

Denham Described

A History of Denham Golf Club
1910 - 1992

Published in a limited edition
of 750 copies
of which 82 copies are for the Sponsors

Copy No.

154

Grant Books, Worcestershire
1992

Contents

Acknowledgements

THE trouble with thanking members who have provided information and suggestions over the last two years is that someone immensely worthy is almost certain to be left out and I shall be wincing at the sight of him, or her, for ever after. However, here goes.

For the achievements of the lady members I was fortunate in being able at various times to call on Mary Braithwaite, Barbara Fox, Meg Moeran, Barbara Hicks, Carol Ritchie, Sue Lang and the late Mrs Whitaker. The text has been greatly enhanced by Nicola Hampel's charming pen and ink drawings. John Woodbridge, who was consulted early on about his family connections with Denham Golf Club, had also, alas, died before the book was finished. Carl Chronander, who must be the senior member still playing, was also most helpful.

One of the first to give aid was Bill Sloley, whose recollections of Denham before and after the Second World War were invaluable. Donald Steel and John Sheridan could be relied upon to confirm or correct impressions of most events and trends in the club's post-war existence. So indeed could Nigel Hague.

I am indebted to John McCallum for allowing me to quote freely from his book *Life with Googie* where it covers their residence in The Mirrie in the 1950s; and to John Way, grandson of Roger Way, for the loan of a family cuttings book.

Robin Marshall and Malcolm Thomas confirmed my own memories of the link between Denham and rugby football, which was a relief; and to any one looking for a sub-committee, I can cordially recommend one comprising Robert Walker, Donald MacKeith, and Jeff Payne (appointed to work out how this book was to be published) as a model of positive thinking.

John Henderson took a kindly interest in the book from the outset and was a source of encouragement in many ways. Between them, he and his father, Walter, had a record of over 50 years almost uninterrupted service on the committee or the board.

Derek Graham could not have been more cooperative, always giving prompt answers to my queries despite the many other calls on a hard-working secretary, and Bob Fenning (Archivist of the Year, if I had a vote) saw that I had all the relevant files. I also much appreciate his writing contributions.

A.C.M. Croome, who later describes a round at Denham in 1926, needs an introduction. A renowned figure in the sporting world for many years, he died in 1930.

Arthur Croome played cricket for Gloucestershire (with Dr W.G. Grace) and, though seriously injured in 1887 when impaling himself on the railings while fielding at Old Trafford, recovered to play several more years for Gloucestershire and then, in the last years of the century, to captain Berkshire.

He was also a fine golfer, hurdler and skater and was one of the founders of the Oxford and Cambridge Golfing Society. He was the society's honorary secretary until 1919 when he became captain. The Croome Shield for foursomes representing the Oxford and Cambridge colleges has been a time-honoured curtain-raiser to the President's Putter.

For some years Croome was a master at Radley before becoming a full-time author and journalist. He was the cricket correspondent of *The Times* (when Bernard Darwin was the golf correspondent) and he wrote about golf in the *Morning Post*. He would have looked at Denham with the critical eye of the golf course architect. He was part-designer of only one course but that is Liphook, a splendid legacy for posterity.

Original colour photographs were taken by Michael Hobbs and Dave Marriott and some early illustrations come from the Hobbs Golf Collection. Fred Hawtree provided the photographs of the course in 1925 and 1955. Other material comes from the archives of Denham Golf Club.

M.M.

Foreword

Donald Steel

WITHOUT Denham Golf Club, I would have had only half a life. Ever since the age of five or six, it has been my second home and, if that implies accusations of a misspent youth, I gratefully plead guilty.

My earliest memory is of the course shrouded in wartime barbed wire with the mound on the right of the 4th hole housing a pill box and a fence running from the 4th green, up the lefthand side of the 18th fairway, and down to what is now the 2nd tee.

My father, returning from a Sunday morning game in 1944, recounted how a German aircraft had flown low over the course on its way back from some dastardly mission. However, happier days were just around the corner, easily the happiest and most significant being the appointment of John Sheridan as professional in the summer of 1946.

It is remarkable to think that his yeoman service spans well over half the life of the club. It was entirely due to him that I fell for the game, hook, slice and mashie and I suggest, with a high degree of confidence, that he has contributed substantially to the welfare and enjoyment of every member – man, woman and child. In 46 years, that is quite a boast.

Uppermost, in promoting the air of friendliness at Denham that we have come to accept, has been John's belief that members shouldn't pick and choose their games. He has always maintained that the best way to get to know people – whatever their handicap – is by having a game with them. The Sheridan Salvers provide his way of putting theory into practice.

What sets Denham apart from other clubs is that the emphasis is on playing golf and having fun at the same time. By insisting on that, as well as fostering foursomes, John will leave a lasting legacy but what helps to make Denham unique is that we have the ideal course and clubhouse to generate the correct ambience.

One other figure, who was equally influential in building up our heritage in the post-war era, was Harry Harrison who 'volunteered' as honorary secretary at about the same time as John's appointment as professional. Whilst insisting on maintaining the best traditions of golf club life, he, nevertheless, realised that the future lay in the hands of the young. In pre-war days, Denham had few young members and the standard of play wasn't particularly high but, between them, Harry and John, in contrasting roles, shaped a different Denham, a better Denham, a Denham whose members became anxious to preserve their good fortune.

It is a joy to me that the history of the club has now been officially written. It is an even greater joy that this labour of love has been mainly performed by Michael Melford – such a source of help when I ventured forth on a career with the *Sunday Telegraph* in 1961.

Those who know Michael recognise a man of good humour and gentle wit, qualities which have guided his approach to this important task. Research has formed a major part of the job in which we also salute the sterling assistance of Bob Fenning. In a work of this nature, deciding what to leave out is as difficult as what to include but, without proper direction, histories can be a stodgy recital of facts which render them unreadable.

As you might expect, the Denham history has avoided all such pitfalls and, in congratulating Michael on making ours an outstanding success, I am sure to express the gratitude of all members. Michael's innate modesty means that there is no mention of himself but I have had many rounds in his company and an incident from one of them supplies a fitting footnote.

On the occasion in question, Michael's wooden club second shot to the 3rd hole flew straight, bounced short and rolled within inches of the flag only to scale the slope at the back of the green and possess just sufficient steam to topple over the edge.

In some, such injustice would have prompted a display of unseemly temperament. But not Michael. His comment was characteristically reproachful, the epitome of restraint. 'Oh Lord', he said, 'the game is hard enough without hitting one out of the middle of the club.'

Donald Steel (right) *before the final of the 1982 President's Putter. He beat Jamie Warman on the 19th. Col. Tony Duncan holds the putter*

1 Recruitment

IT IS indisputable that Denham Golf Club was opened for play on 29 May 1911, a fortnight after the first members were elected, and one has to accept that it had been conceived at a meeting of the seven founders at the Savay Farm as recently as 10 August 1910. Even allowing for the fact that the first players were asked to make piles of stones beside the fairways to be collected by a stone-wallah with a horse and cart, this seems an extraordinarily brief period of gestation, by modern thinking anyhow.

The archives begin only in December 1910 and one is left to guess at the reasons which prompted the seven good men to found a golf club. The seven, who took the first shares in the company on 20 December, were described in the first register as:

Alfred Henry Tarleton of Breakspear, described as Esquire MVO, who was the first chairman;

Major Charles Wyld, of The Tile House, Denham, His Majesty's Army (retired list);

Richard Henry Morten, of the Savoy, Denham (as Savay Farm was often called,) Gentleman Farmer;

Thomas Doodputlee McMeekin, of The Thatched House, Gerrards Cross, Gentleman;

John Calvert Hibbert, of Highfield House, Uxbridge, Banker;

Major Benjamin Irby Way, of Denham Place, His Majesty's Army (retired list);

William Haldane Porter, of Quenby, Gerrards Cross, Barrister at Law, HM Inspector at the Home Office under the Aliens Act.

By a coincidence these words are being written on what, in 1910, was part of Mr Haldane Porter's property.

To these was soon added Francis Charles Woodbridge, solicitor of The Briars, Gerrards Cross. According to the late John Woodbridge, his uncle was not a golfer but he was the first of the family which was to have a considerable influence on the club's affairs. In January William George Blakemore, of Garston Lodge, Gerrards Cross, was asked if he would be the auditor. He accepted and Blakemore and Elgar remain the club's auditors in the 1990s, as Turberville Woodbridge remain the solicitors.

While a picture begins to form of a club efficiently organised by local landowners, the building-up of a reputable and useful membership seems to have been given priority. Thus, one of the first to receive a director's nomination was Henry James Buckmaster, then of Marsham Lodge, Gerrards Cross, the successful founder of Buck's Club. At the time he was married to Gladys Cooper, the great beauty of the London theatre in those days. Their daughter was to become Mrs Robert Morley.

Another elected in the first weeks of the club was Gerald du Maurier, shortly to become one of the great actor-managers of the day. He was also a very good golfer. Aged 38 he had just taken over Wyndham's Theatre in conjunction with Frank Curzon whose subsequent successes included winning the 1927 Derby with Call Boy.

Gerald du Maurier was the son of George, the famous artist of *Punch* and the author of *Trilby*. He was the father of Daphne du Maurier, the novelist. At this time he lived at Croxley Green and was already a member of Northwood. He had many successes ahead of him, one in 1921 as Bulldog Drummond, and he had many charitable interests. He was president of the Actors Orphanage from 1914 and was knighted in the New Year Honours of 1922. If the stage was still not quite accepted as a profession of distinction, Gerald du Maurier provided the touch of charm and respectability which completed the transformation.

Sir Gerald du Maurier

Another actor elected was Louis Goodrich, a prominent member of the Green Room Club who had had a full and varied life. Born at the Royal Military College, Sandhurst, the son of Major-General E. Abbot Anderson, he was originally intended for the Army but became a land surveyor in what were then called the Colonies, a farmer in British Columbia and a tea planter in Ceylon. He was also an amateur actor and eventually went on the professional stage in New York. For 10 years thereafter he was on the London stage before serving in the Army throughout the 1914–18 War.

In the pre-war days many of Denham's early members came from the Services and there were also two eminent cricketers. B.J.T. Bosanquet had played in seven Test matches for England, all against Australia, but it was as the inventor of the googly, the off-break bowled with a leg-break action, that he became famous. It is still called the 'bosie' in Australia.

When Bosanquet had played in his last Test match, at Headingley in 1905, the England captain had been the Hon. F.S. Jackson, who made 144 not out.

The founding fathers of Denham could scarcely have approached a more distinguished Englishman than Stanley Jackson. Though prevented from going on tours by business commitments he had played 20 times for England and had played for Yorkshire until 1907. The son of Lord Allerton, who had been in the Cabinet during Lord Salisbury's second government, he had captained Harrow, where he had Winston Churchill as a fag, and Cambridge (not Yorkshire, for Lord Hawke did not retire until 1910). During the 1914–18 war he was to raise a West Yorkshire Regiment which he commanded himself. In 1915 he became the Unionist MP for Howden. In 1922, when he was president of MCC, he became financial secretary to the War Office and chairman of the Unionist Party.

In 1927 Lieut. Colonel the Right Hon. Sir Stanley Jackson was appointed Governor of Bengal. The committee of Denham Golf Club instructed the secretary to write to him congratulating him on his appointment and sending him their best wishes. The latter may be said to have been badly needed. Not long after he arrived in Calcutta, Sir Stanley had to survive an attempt to assassinate him.

B.J.T. Bosanquet

During the Second World War his London home was bombed but in 1946 he was still active as a trustee of MCC, as president of Yorkshire and as chairman of the England selectors who picked Alec Bedser for his first Test match. In the following year he died aged 76.

Despite a full public life Sir Stanley had been one of the finest all-round games players of the age. Before he joined Denham in 1911 he had been a member of Ganton, where he was plus two, and Alwoodley. A card exists showing that in March 1922 he had a gross 70 at Denham where he was still plus one at the age of 51.

Sir Stanley Jackson

In the early days there were three types of membership – full golf, provisional golf and tennis. There were four lawn tennis courts, two on what is now the putting green behind the club house, two where the Artisans'

	Bogey.	Length in yds.	Score.	Bogey Result.		Bogey.	Length in yds.	Score.	Bogey Result.
1	4	353	4	0	10	5	400	4	+
2	4	353	5	–	11	4	374	3	+
3	5	412	5	0	12	3	132	3	0
4	5	401	4	+	13	5	528	5	0
5	4	221	4	0	14	5	424	4	+
6	5	382	5	0	15	5	429	3	+
7	5	423	4	+	16	3	105	3	0
8	3	176	3	0	17	4	356	4	0
9	5	438	3	+	18	5	398	4	+
	40	3,159	37			39	3,147	33	

DENHAM GOLF CLUB.

Name of Player... *Hon. F.S. Jackson* ... Date... *11th March 1922*

Total Length, 6,306 yards.
Won: Lost: Halved:

In .. 33
Out .. 37
Total .. 70
Handicap .. +1
Nett .. 71

Jackson's gross 70

clubhouse now stands. The entrance fee settled down at 10 guineas, though it was reduced or waived for directors' nominations. The subscription was 6 guineas. Green fees were 3s 6d ($17\frac{1}{2}$p) per day if playing with a member, 5s (25p) if introduced by letter. But even Bob Fenning, whose spells as secretary of the club in the 1970s and 1980s make him profoundly knowledgeable on the mechanics of it, confesses to finding parts of the early archives pretty baffling.

'It is impossible', he says, 'to relate the election of members to the total numbers. According to the candidates' book only 63 names are recorded as elected in 1911 but on 21 November, 1911 a lady candidate was placed on the waiting list. Of the 63, the last, a Mr W.W. Bond, of Greythorpe, Gerrards Cross, was proposed on Christmas Day and elected a full member on December 28. One interpretation is that a provisional member was one who did not have a 10s share and could not vote. But there were 300 10s shares so it is difficult to see why there were provisional members unless the committee were in doubt.' (But this can scarcely explain the election, in 1913 as only a provisional member, of Lieut. General the Hon. Sir Frederick William Stopford KCMG, KCVO, CB.)

New members were proposed and seconded but there was no certainty that the proposers and seconders had been proposed and seconded themselves. An elegant copperplate writing graces the early pages of the minute book but the chairman's agenda book provides a stiffer test. On the left-hand page the topic to be discussed is clear enough. On the opposite page, however, the action taken is in handwriting which taxes the reader's ingenuity. Sometimes, too, an intriguing item on the agenda such as the negotiations with the railway company whets your curiosity but when you look on the other page for enlightenment, all you get is 'noted'.

In July 1911 there is mention on the left-hand page of a letter from Miss du Cane, lady-in-waiting to HH Princess Victoria of Schleswig Holstein. On the right-hand page this only earned a laconic 'read'. This was doubtless not unconnected with the fact that the first president of the club was Prince Albert of Schleswig Holstein, who had been captain of Sunningdale in 1912. But the first mention of him in the committee minutes, or elsewhere in the archives, is of his resignation. In the minutes of the committee meeting on 31 October 1914 is just the formal statement, 'The resignation of the President, Prince Albert of Schleswig Holstein was accepted.' Sadly it was one of many resignations which the prince, a great admirer of Britain and the British, had to make in 1914.

The archives leave a lot of questions open to speculation as to what inspired the formation of a golf club on this site. Was it something which the seven founders, or some of the seven, had long been considering? Were they all passionately keen golfers? (Several, in fact, did not play.) Clearly Major Way, who owned the land, must have played a decisive part. Did the idea grow on him as he looked out of the front windows of Denham Place at the hill opposite and thought that its gravel subsoil would be better suited as a well-drained golf course than as somewhat reluctant farming land? Did he have any idea that he and the other six were starting something which would still be giving so much pleasure to so many 80 years later? They certainly seem to have followed the basic, if expensive, precept in the creation of golf courses – that if you are going to do it, you must do it properly, for you are starting something which, you hope, will live in perpetuity – and will be even more expensive to amend later.

The choice of architect for the golf course followed this precept most faithfully, for it fell on H.S. Colt, widely considered one of the best of the age – and not only in England. How it fell on him is not clear, for apart from a note in the chairman's agenda book for 11 September 1911, authorising the payment of £13 to H.S. Colt Esquire, there is no reference to him anywhere in the early records or to the building of the golf course.

Harry Colt

In golfing circles, however, it is no secret that Harry Colt designed Denham. Donald Steel, himself one of the most respected golf course architects of today, has written:

> Colt, born in 1869, played much of his early golf at St Andrews and his admiration for the Old Course undoubtedly influenced his concepts of design. These became known after he had left Cambridge and was working as a solicitor in Hastings. It was during this period that he designed Rye but he did not become fully engaged in this new career until 1900 when he was made the first secretary of Sunningdale where he remained for 12 years.
>
> He later became so famous in the golfing world as an architect that the younger generation may tend to think of him solely in this role, but Colt was also a fine golfer who played for England in 1908, beside reaching the semi-final of the 1906 Amateur Championship at Hoylake and the sixth round in two other years.

As well as Rye and Denham, Harry Colt designed a host of courses including Royal Portrush, Moor Park, Northampton County, the New Course at Sunningdale, Trevose, the Eden Course at St Andrews, Stoke Poges and (with his partners of later years, C.H. Alison and J.S.F. Morrison), Wentworth. He went to Holland to design the Kennemer course and in 1913 to the United States 'during a brief but critical period in the lengthy construction of Pine Valley'.

In his book *Sheridan of Sunningdale* James Sheridan, the much-loved caddiemaster and father, of course, of John Sheridan, referred to Colt as 'a great and wonderful man'.

It is a tribute to Colt, who lived until 1951, that no basic change has been made to the course at Denham, in spite of the upsets of two World Wars. He must have been hard at work during the winter of 1910–11, as was W.J. Page, the builder who was turning the old farmhouse and barn into a clubhouse. His firm of W.J. Page & Son Ltd still thrives in Station Approach, Northwood. Payments to Page totalling £2,575, a few hundred pounds at a time, were still being made in 1912, a year after the course was open. Other payments for building work included £488 to a certain J. Bailey.

According to the minutes of the second meeting (statutory) of the

GOLF CLUB HOUSE, DENHAM.   MR. MELVILLE SETH-WARD, F.R.I.B.A., ARCHITECT.

Denham Golf Club Ltd, it was held at Hill Barn farm, Denham on 25 March 1911. As the new clubhouse was growing out of a farm and a barn on a hill, this presumably was the original farm's name. Thereafter meetings were held in 'the Club House'. Charlie Stone, who was the locker room attendant until the 1970s, after working for many years on the course and in the bar, used to say that his mother had been born in the 1850s in the farmhouse which in modern times has been the ladies' locker room and now houses the secretary's office and the committee room.

The first meeting of directors was, like the one in 1910 which decided to form a golf club, at 'The Savoy', as Savay Farm was still referred to not infrequently. Savay Farm it is on present-day maps but Savoy seems to have been its name in the Middle Ages. Whatever it is called, it is a house with a history of its own.

In his book *Companion into Buckinghamshire* Maxwell Fraser writes: 'The most interesting house in the district is the Savoy on the banks of the Colne, a moated house incorporating the remains of an aisled hall from the 14th century.'

Reginald T.W. Hammond in *The Complete Thames Valley and Chilterns* goes further:

Just north of Denham is Savay Farm, one of the oldest and most interesting domestic houses in England still in daily use. It dates from the 13th century and was extended in the 15th and 16th centuries. In the 1930s Savay Farm was the home of Sir Oswald Mosley, whose first wife, Lady Cynthia, also a Labour MP, was buried there. Desecration of the grave in 1970 caused the remains to be reinterred in the village churchyard. The house is privately owned. During the Second World War Savay Farm was used as a centre for experiments in chemical warfare and was frequently visited by Winston Churchill.

Churchill was not the first Prime Minister to have visited Savay Farm. In Nicholas Mosley's moving book, about his parents and his own boyhood at Savay Farm, there are pictures of the turbulent social life there in the 1920s and 1930s and Ramsay McDonald is shown writing a major speech there when Prime Minister.

The legend that Sir Oswald Mosley once applied unsuccessfully for membership of Denham Golf Club is confirmed in the committee minutes of April 1928. When he was proposed, he had already moved from the Conservative to the Labour Party but had not yet reached the lofty levels of unpopularity which he attained in the 1930s as the black-shirted leader of the British Union of Fascists. Indeed, in the following year of 1929 he became Chancellor of the Duchy of Lancaster in the Labour Government.

He was thus still relatively respectable when the Denham committee addressed itself to his application for membership. The chairman, H.G. Muskett, laid before the meeting a letter to the secretary signed by 41 members saying 'without wishing to make any reflections, political or social, about this gentleman, we believe that it will not be in the best interests of the Club that he should be elected.'

The chairman then asked each member of the committee for his views. It was finally agreed that 'it was manifest that should this election be by ballot Mr Mosley [he had not yet inherited the baronetcy] would fail to be elected. It was resolved

Mosley at the peak of his influence in 1936

unanimously that it be postponed as the best course to adopt in the true interests of the Club, giving the Candidate the opportunity of withdrawing his application.'

Two members of the committee undertook to convey the decision to the proposer, a peer, and the seconder, a general.

But that was all in the future. Whereas in the 1930s the respective owners of Savay Farm and Denham Place, Mosley and Sir Robert Vansittart, whose lands marched on each other, were very far from being at one, Richard Morten and Major Way were at the very heart of the infant golf club's affairs.

The Way family, which still has three members of Denham, was, according to *Highways and Byways in Buckinghamshire* by Clement Shorter, of Somerset and Devon origin. Denham Place and its estate came into the family through Abigail Hill who married Lewis Way in the 17th century. Her father, Sir Roger Hill, MP for Amersham, bought the manor of Denham in 1670 and built Denham Place in 1676. His elder daughter inherited it and eventually it passed to her sister.

The debt owed by the club to the Way family is beyond measure – for making the land available in the first place, as benevolent landlords for over 30 years, and then for allowing the club to buy the freehold at well below market value.

2 Expansion

A N ALMOST essential requirement for a golf club in the days before motor cars became commonplace was an adjacent railway station, though in the 1990s Denham Golf Club must be unique, or very near it, in still having one bearing its name. Few clubs in the neighbourhood were not near a railway. You do not have to be in your dotage to have walked from Carpenders Park Station across a field of bluebells to the Oxhey Golf Club, now long gone. From Preston Road it was barely 100 yards to the equally defunct Harrow Golf Club. The Beaconsfield clubhouse is not much more than a long putt from the Seer Green and Jordans Station which opened on New Year's Day 1915 – and so on.

An illustrated book on the Great Western and Great Central Railways says that it was not until the 1930s that commuters using Denham Golf Club Station outnumbered golfers. Thus it was in the interests of both the railway and the golf club that the Halt should be established, though the company did make a condition for opening the station that a given number of tickets was issued each week.

The 'Platform' to give it its first name, was opened in August 1912 and soon became a 'Halt'. Before and after its opening, the negotiations seem to have been conducted in an admirable spirit of cooperation, which may have been born a few years earlier when the line to Gerrards Cross and parts west was driven through the Way family's land.

One topic for negotiation had been the construction of a footpath to the Halt. The two platforms were not then directly opposite each other, the up-platform being nearer London. The projected footpath ran straight on to the up-platform from the point where the gravel road across the 11th runs out of the gate and turns right.

In March 1914 the golf club was in a strong enough position to write to the railway asking it to stop the 1.25pm train from Paddington at the Golf Club Halt,

The station in 1992

9

Vardon putting on the 11th green at Denham

At both Denham and Fulwell, a strong, fitful wind prevailed, but a comparison of experiences of people who attended either place indicated that the Denham brigade had the worst of the weather. There, the showers of hail and rain early in the day were very severe, and they left so much casual water on the greens that for a time it was difficult to discover a line that gave a putt to the hole without water intervening.

The gravel subsoil soon absorbed most of the moisture, but the turf was naturally left somewhat soft. Denham, however, is a fine course; every hole has a character of its own, and many of the second shots afford scope for the best golf that champions can supply. Its only faults are the faults of newness.

Most of the better-known players started late. W.H. Horne, formerly of Chertsey but now unattached, led at the end of 18 holes with a score of 75, Harry Vardon, J.B. Batley, Joshua Taylor, and G. Cawkwell coming next with 77 each. In the afternoon, Joshua Taylor led the field for a long time with a total of 157. He looked like doing the second round in another 77, but, at the fifteenth hole, he hit the trees which he tried to carry with his brassie shot and went out of bounds. The hole cost him 7. Later, Batley arrived with a score of 75, making his aggregate 152. Except that he took eight putts on the first three greens, Batley played fine golf all day; his approaches were especially good and he holed just one long putt in each round.

Vardon came in with a 75, and so equalled Batley's total. Vardon was rather slack on the outward journey in the afternoon, and was bunkered twice from pulled shots, although he had bad luck at the fifth, a hole of 200 yards, at which he made a splendid drive

which just caught the bank of the bunker and dropped into the hazard. He cut it very fine so as to try and finish near the flag, and a difference of a few inches in the flight would have put him nicely on the green. He went out in 41. Coming home, he showed his best form, and, by holing a long putt on the home green, he accomplished a score of 34 for the last nine holes. His partner had rounds of 114 and 99!

James Braid kept a good line except from three tees, and, although he missed two short putts in the morning, his putting was steady for the greater part. He had a chance of tying with the leaders, but pulled his drive to the seventeenth and lost his ball. Horne went completely off his short game in the afternoon and took 83. Leading scores:

Harry Vardon, South Herts	77	75	152
J.B. Batley, Bushey Hall	77	75	152
James Braid, Walton Heath	78	76	154
Tom Ball, Raynes Park	79	76	155
Joshua Taylor, Acton	77	80	157
C.H. Mayo, Burhill	78	80	158
W.H. Horne, unattached	75	83	158
J. Sidey, Bramshot	79	80	159
G. Cawkwell, Guildford	77	82	159
Ernest Jones, Chislehurst	79	80	159
Jack White, Sunningdale	83	77	160
A. Catlin, Old Fold Manor	78	83	161

The above qualified Catlin after a tie with Ayton and Bradbeer.

L. Ayton, Bishops Stortford	80	81	161
J. Bradbeer, Porters Park	82	79	161
J.C. Lonie, Bromley & Bickley	82	80	162
P. Grace, Berkhamsted	83	79	162
A. Bellworthy, West Herts	82	80	162

a request which seems to have met with a friendly acknowledgment. The last correspondence before the war was 're sand from Bude', but the outcome of that, and the stopping of the 1.25, seems to have been lost in the fog of war.

During 1911 the club, from a standing start, made remarkable progress, a tribute no doubt to the public relations of the directors. Societies, mostly called associations in those days, were soon asking if they could play their annual tournament at Denham.

On 8 January 1912 the first AGM of the club was held. The chairman, Mr Tarleton, explained that the directors had waited for this before electing a captain and committee. J.C. Hibbert, proposed by the chairman and seconded by Major Way and well known in the Uxbridge area as a golfer and cricketer, was then installed as the first captain. A committee of seven was elected – R.L. Alderson, M.J. Hall, C. de W. Kitcat, D.C. Lee, A.S. Lucy, John Mews and B.P. Stedall. At the next meeting later in January three sub-committees were elected – house, green, and competition and handicap. In March Mrs Peel-Smith became the first lady captain.

The competition and handicap sub-committee was soon in action, advising the club committee that they did not recommend a professional competition on the course this year, as the PGA had requested. There must have been some doubt too about the readiness of the clubhouse.

In 1913, however, the PGA tried again, specifying that that they would like half their Southern section to play their qualifying rounds of *The Sphere* and *Tatler* Cup and the Tooting Bec Challenge Cup at Denham on 7 May 1913. Mr Haldane Porter, seconded by Mr McMeekin, proposed that the PGA should be allowed to go ahead and the committee, far from yielding reluctantly, recommended that a sum of money (£15) should be granted by the directors as prizes and that lunch and tea should be provided for players, sponsors and the press. The day seems to have been a great success and warm letters of thanks were received from both the PGA and the proprietors of *The Sphere* and *Tatler*.

One of the first societies to ask to play at Denham, probably at the suggestion of Mr Haldane Porter, was the Home Office G.S. who played their competition there on the King's Birthday in 1912. The lady captain asked permission for matches against West Drayton and Stoke Poges. The club again agreed to pay for lunch and tea. The Bar G.S. was one of the first to play a match against Denham, a fixture still going strong in the 1990s.

At the first recorded meeting of the company on 30 January 1911, Richard Morten, in his own house 'The Savoy', acted as hon. secretary. He seems to have been largely responsible for the tennis of which he became the first captain. One of the first two tennis members was Freddie Grisewood, who was to become one of the best known broadcasters on BBC radio when it began in the early 1920s. Mr Tarleton took the chair, as he did at almost every meeting of the company until the war broke out in 1914. Mr Woodbridge, the solicitor, acted as assistant hon. secretary.

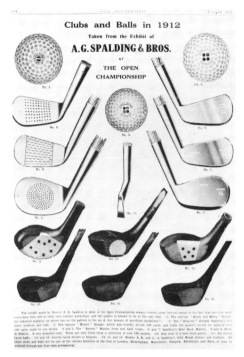

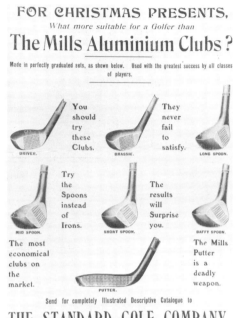

Some of the clubs that early Denham members had to choose from

Note that metal woods are not a modern invention

By the end of 1911 Major W.E.S. Tyler was established as secretary of both club and company. At the 50th anniversary dinner in 1960 Jack Moir referred to the earlier secretaries as having been honorary. Some were, but Major Tyler is shown as receiving a salary of £150 a year from 11 April 1911. It had risen to £225 by the outbreak of war. One of the first items dealt with by the greens committee had been 'referred to pro', so it seems that J. Turner had been appointed quite early on. In June 1912 he was granted £10 towards his expenses in attending the Open Championship at Muirfield. He was also the greenkeeper, though when he left in 1913 the two jobs were separated.

A long-serving member of the staff who survived nearly every one else involved in the club's earliest years was the caddiemaster Wyatt. Appointed at 18 to 20s a week, before the course opened in May 1911, he was still around in the Second World War when the possession of the cottage in which he lived became an issue during the purchase of the course from the Way family.

Early in his reign the committee met a modest request for a contribution to the Caddies Association. They followed this up by asking members to

contribute 2s 6d a head (12½p) to a fund for the purchase of mackintosh capes or coats for caddies, to be the property of the club but to be taken out by caddies when the weather required.

Even though the club was not a year old in playing terms, Major Tyler was soon launched on what is no doubt that age-old springtime occupation of golf club secretaries, the pursuit of unpaid subscriptions. The committee set a date, 1 May, after which the offender would be struck off, and they held to it unless there was a clearly genuine reason such as illness, which had caused the omission. They stood firm, too, on other infringements of the club's rules but were prepared to review the rules if members wanted it. Thus when a member wanted to put up a 'Cottage to Let' notice, they said they were unable to allow this under existing rules but were prepared to look for ways in which it might be acceptable in future.

They could be quite tough, as when one member, given several previous warnings, overran the deadline by two days. They returned his cheque. They politely rejected the suggestion on behalf of a physician to the Royal Family 'that he should be ranked for subscription purposes with serving officers'. They also turned down a suggestion that provisional members, who in effect were five-day members, might play on Saturday and Sunday if they paid a green fee of 2s 6d. They considered making the American naval attaché, who was 'desirous of joining', an honorary member but eventually ranked him with British serving officers.

When its owner was not busy insuring the club, notably against suffragettes, the long arm of Major Tyler reached out to bring off one coup. He discovered that a member in the foreign category was back in England and had just won a competition. The major ran him down working at Scotland Yard and the committee asked him for the balance of the year's subscription.

In 1913 the club was asked by the British Olympic Committee to run a competition to raise funds for the next Games which should have taken place in 1916 in Berlin. This one was left on the table. Nor were they sympathetic with the Uxbridge Boy Scouts, who wanted to use the course for manoeuvres after dark.

One rule not infrequently broken was that which limited the introduction of the same visitor to six times a year. The record was undoubtedly held by a Mr Trower who came 17 times. The secretary was also instructed to write to the member who had introduced a Miss Dare nine times, pointing out the breach of rules, though if this was Miss Zena or Miss Phyllis Dare, who were picture postcard beauties of the day, one might think that it would have been a matter for commendation rather than censure.

It was a year or two before the club house, the furnishing of which was the responsibility of Messrs Morten and McMeekin, was geared to accommodate all who wished to come. The first plan of the architect Melville Seth-Ward was rejected as too expensive. His second was basically what existed in modern times before the handsome extensions of the late 1980s. He himself presented the club with the Irish yews in the front court.

There was at first no accommodation for the staff and the first steward lived for a time in what had been the former farmhouse. The opening hours for the bar were settled at between 9am and 11pm.

Meanwhile Mrs Peel-Smith and the ladies committee were given a fair measure of autonomy and seem to have made good progress in starting their own competitions and in building a fixture list. By the end of 1913, however, the number of players on the course, both male and female, was beginning to worry the main committee and some reports of lady members and their guests 'cutting up the course and not replacing divots' added to their concern. These were passed on to the lady captain for action, which was duly taken where possible, but requests from the Ladies Medical G.A. and the Ladies Legal G.A. to play on the course were turned down. The membership hereabouts was 350–375 men, 50 ladies.

Early in 1914 Mr Haldane Porter, captain in 1913, proposed that no lady's name be placed on the waiting list for full membership unless she had a LGU handicap of 16. This was carried unanimously, as was the recommendation of the green committee that all the membership lists be closed, the committee to have discretion to elect any candidate 'who may be considered desirable'.

A year before, the concern in some quarters had been about the club's financial position. This was dispelled at the AGM by the chairman. Mr Tarleton, who took this opportunity of stating most emphatically that there was no foundation for these rumours and the financial position was absolutely satisfactory. 'This is not a proprietary Club', he went on, 'so that all the profits will be devoted to the improvement of the Course and Club and I have every faith and confidence in the future of the Club.'

Early in 1912 Mr Tarleton had given a silver challenge cup for competition annually, asking the competition committee to decide the conditions under which it should be played. The first winner in 1912 was E.J. Sissons.

Ernest Sissons became a force in the club in a short time. A member of the Stock Exchange, he had still been living in Sevenoaks when in October 1911 he joined Denham through the director's nomination of Mr McMeekin. He was already a member of Littlestone and Sevenoaks. He later moved house to Gerrards Cross, was on the committee of Denham in 1913 and in 1914, proposed by Mr Haldane Porter and seconded by Mr Hibbert, he became the club's third captain.

By now ranks were being given in the minutes of committee meetings. Officers on the reserve list were presumably being put in a greater state of readiness. In June 1914 Commander Tarleton was still in the chair, though Captain Charles Wyld sometimes deputised for him. Major B.I. Way was now Lieut. Colonel Way.

Though the committee took on more matches in 1914, such as those against Consolidated Goldfields and the Naval and Military Club, and allowed the London Municipal G.S. the use of the course on the usual terms of 2s 6d per head, there were real worries about over-crowding at weekends.

When the president of the Officers Mess of the RAMC asked if members of the mess could be accepted as Service members on payment of a Mess subscription of 40 guineas a year, the committee regretted that the course was already sufficiently crowded. In just over three years since the first golf ball was struck on the course Denham had had a considerable success and had to be wary of problems which might come out of it. Inside the clubhouse no such self-discipline was required.

The gifts to the club began with what could almost be called a spate of grandfather clocks, anyhow two of them. In April 1912 Mr E.B. Robinson had started the collection of animal souvenirs in the dining room with a moose's head. Colonel Way followed with a set of horns, Mr G.M. Nichols with two sets of horns. Unfortunately during the war the moose had to go. Mr Robinson wrote to ask whether he might be allowed to exchange it for another head. It seems that the donor who had shot the moose had been killed in action and his relatives were anxious to have the head back.

This was obviously a blow to those members who had grown fond of the moose but the committee steeled themselves and agreed to the substitution.

More heads followed and Colonel Way contributed the wonderfully practical gift of 2,000 trees but Mr Woodbine Parish nipped in with a condor skin before the war put an end to the generosity. Until 1919, it seems, no one had any mooses or condors to spare.

3 War Footing

TO A new golf club only just over three years old, the outbreak of war on 4 August 1914 was inevitably a severe blow which halted, and in some respects put into reverse, the momentum of previous years. From having a growing waiting list, the club had to adjust itself to accepting a lot of resignations from members who did not see themselves playing much golf in the foreseeable future at Denham or elsewhere. Economies were going to be needed and subscriptions reduced. A heavy burden was going to lie with those who took up the administrative responsibilities.

Almost at once the club lost two stalwarts of its early days. The leader of the seven founders, Commander Tarleton, who as chairman had scarcely missed a committee meeting hitherto, soon wrote to say that his work at the Admiralty would prevent him from attending meetings during the war. He asked to resign as a director. His resignation was not accepted and he was twice re-elected when his span as a director was up. In 1918 he was elected president of the club, a position he held until his death in June 1922.

The secretary, Major Tyler, was also called back to the colours at the outbreak of war but remained in touch and in a letter from Western Command at Chester he added a revealing footnote. His clerk at Western Command, he said, was 'not a Reeves'. This established for the reader of the minute book that Charles Reeves, who soon became referred to as the acting secretary, was the owner of the splendid copperplate writing in the book. Reeves clearly played an invaluable part in the running of the club until he was called up in the spring of 1917.

Then, however, the club had a bit of luck. Within a few weeks Major Tyler was demobilised. He informed the committee that he thought he was about to be appointed secretary of the St James Club in London but hoped that he would be free on Sundays to help out at Denham until the end of the war. At this news, cheering must have broken out among the directors.

The major was as good as his word and hung on until November 1918 when he wrote that owing to the pressure of other work he found himself unable to continue coming to Denham every Sunday. He had been advised that, in the interests of his health, it was necessary for him to have one day a week off and with great regret he was compelled to tender his resignation.

With respect to Major Tyler, who seems to have been a thoroughly good egg, this is a relief to the reader of the minute book, for as the Sundays passed, the strain on the Major was reflected in his handwriting, which became ever less legible.

The burden of running the club, which became increasingly heavy from the middle of 1917, fell largely on Mr Haldane Porter as chairman and on the captains, of whom there were only two during the War. Mr Sissons, captain in 1914, was re-elected for 1915 after which Ernest Radley took over.

Mr Radley was not a local resident – his address is given as the New Oxford and Cambridge Club and later as Albert Hall Mansions – but his was one of the first names in the members book in June 1911. He had previously been a member of Bramshott Golf Club. The cynic might say that anyone who was landed with such a job in a war was bound to be re-elected because no one else wanted it, but Mr Radley seems to have satisfied one and all in his five years as captain of Denham. The directors, the founders, were also re-elected whenever their stint ended until 1922. Mr Skidmore, manager of Barclay's Bank, Uxbridge, continued as hon. treasurer, and Blackmore & Co as auditors.

Apart from the departure of Major Tyler, the war soon brought a number of changes in the daily running of the club. Four of the ground staff enlisted – and were guaranteed an income until their Army pay began coming through. There were many resignations from members. Several rules were relaxed, notably Rule 33 which limited the introduction of the same guest to six times a year. Provisional members were now allowed to play on Saturdays and Sundays on payment of a green fee. When the club sounded out eight men and 19 ladies on the provisional list on whether they still wished to take up membership from 1 January 1915, only one man and eight ladies said that they did.

Many resignations were accompanied by a query as to whether members would be able to rejoin without entrance fee after the war. Economies were needed but members and others seem to have been very fairly treated, with each case judged on its merits.

Not all resignations were accepted with regret. One member and his wife resigned in protest at a charge of 1s 3d (6¼p) for a bread and cheese lunch.

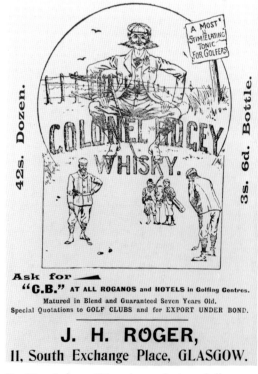

Doubtless there would have been a shortage of all brands of whisky, including this brand of the time

The accounts, up to the end of 1914, showed a profit of £1,800 despite five months of war but there had been a falling-off in members and others using the club. The monthly medal was discontinued after only two cards had been returned in September. The autumn meeting was cancelled and new local rules were drawn up for when the scheduled trenches had been dug at the 2nd, 3rd, 4th, 6th, 15th and 18th holes.

Golfers in the Services home on leave were allowed to play twice without payment and afterwards six times on payment of the usual green fee. Some nice distinctions had to be made. A member asked what subscriptions he and his wife had to pay as he was serving in the Royal Engineers in Cornwall and his wife would not be using the club. It was decided that he should pay 10s 6d and she the normal subscription of 2 guineas.

Mr H.J. Corin wrote saying that he was giving his services as a dental surgeon to the Admiralty and going to France every weekend. What should his subscription be? The committee decided that it should be 10s 6d. This became the standard sum for members serving in HM Forces home and abroad for the rest of the war.

Committee meetings continued every month. In April, with Mr Haldane Porter in the chair, Mr Hibbert said that he did not think that the lunches on Saturdays and Sundays were being kept up to standard. He was authorised to tell the steward that he was economising 'a little too much'.

In January 1916 the board of directors suspended the entrance fee, and 28 new full members, male and female, were elected, five from the provisional list. They included Turberville Smith, the solicitor who was to play a big part as captain of the club in the next war. Seven new provisional members were elected, six ladies and a vicar.

Hereabouts the professional, J. Rowlands, who had taken over before the war, was called up but lodged an application for exemption with the local tribunal. He was passed fit. The committee told him that they would take charge of any stock left in his shop and try to sell it for him. The greenkeeper, Flint, was willing to look after the shop on Saturdays and Sundays and to do minor repairs. Rowlands arranged with a firm in London to do repairs needing expertise.

Earlier in 1916 the caddiemaster, R. Wyatt, had been given the job of keeping the garden round the clubhouse in order during the summer. In the autumn he was given employment by the Red Cross Society and went to France. As it happened, Beazley, the ground foreman, had only been passed C2 (labour at home) and had been temporarily sent back by the Army. He undertook to do Wyatt's job on Saturdays and Sundays.

By this time in 1916 the committee were becoming apprehensive about the future. Though the financial position of the club was still said to be very satisfactory, it was felt that some steps should be taken to limit the loss on the house account and to increase the club's income. Thus from 1 January 1917 the entrance fee was restored: 4 guineas for full members, 2 guineas for provisional, and the price of a hot lunch was raised to 3s forthwith.

Throughout the war those running the club seem to have maintained happy relations with military and other establishments in the neighbourhood. This was to stand them in good stead as the pace of events quickened in 1917.

Cadets stationed at the nearby camp were allowed to play golf and tennis at Denham. They and others gave concerts and held dances in the dining room. When Denham Cricket Club asked if the golf club had a second-hand mowing machine for sale at a low figure, the committee found one no longer needed by the greenkeeper and gave it to the cricket club free of charge. They seldom refused a request from the officers at Denham Camp if it was for anything within the committee's powers.

Shortages had already necessitated closing the club at 8pm and potatoes were only served on Saturdays and Sundays but a subject not directly connected with the war was given more space in the minutes of January and February 1917 than any other matter had earned so far. This concerned two members, one lady and one gentleman, who had given two separate addresses in London but were alleged to have been occupying the same house in Gerrards Cross during the previous summer, 'thus causing considerable comment among the members of the club'. The committee considered that 'the fact that such comment was being made endangered the character and interest of the club'. They asked the offending gentleman, who soon after his own election in the previous year had proposed the lady for membership, for an explanation.

It would have been interesting to know what would have happened if the gentleman had said that the lady was his mother or, more gallantly perhaps, his daughter. In his reply, however, he merely said that the 'insinuations' of the committee were without foundation.

The committee, who were doubtless well informed by this time, unanimously came to the conclusion that this explanation was neither adequate nor satisfactory. They asked for his resignation within a week. They got it – and that of the lady – and ended the exchanges on an even higher moral note by returning the couple's subscriptions for 1917.

Back to the war. In April 1917 Charles Reeves – he of the copperplate writing – was called up. Though Mr Blakemore, the auditor, said that his firm would lend someone to look after the accounts until the secretarial post was filled, it was scarcely necessary. In the following month Major Tyler returned, on full time until 1 September when he was to take up the St James appointment, thereafter on Sundays.

Towards the end of June 1917 the club had a nasty scare when two RAMC officers, accompanied by the OC Cadet Wing RFC Denham Camp, took certain measurements in the clubhouse and elsewhere with a view, apparently, to its conversion into a hospital for the camp. No notice of the visit was given, either to the club or to the landlord, Colonel Way. The whisper from friendly sources at the camp was that there was no chance of the club's being requisitioned because the camp authorities thought that it was of such value to them for recreation and for entertaining their friends.

A practice device of the time. Did it work?

Major Tyler, however, pointed out that the final decision lay with Eastern Command and the War Office. He urged the committee to take the threat seriously. This they did, drawing up various plans, the most pessimistic of which would have closed the club altogether.

Colonel Way sent a telegram strongly opposing any take-over and the hospitalisation of Denham Golf Club seems to have soon receded.

In February 1918, however, a much more likely prospect loomed up and a special committee meeting was called to consider a demand from the Bucks War Agricultural Committee (hereinafter BWAC) that the club should plough up 120 acres of land, cultivate it and sow it with spring corn for the 1918 harvest. With the farmer Richard Morten directing the operation, the club willingly agreed to the demand in the interests of the nation and set about minimising its impact on the life of the club.

As early as August 1914 Mr Morten had undertaken to inspect the hay on the course and to sell any which was surplus to requirements. At the AGM in May 1917 the chairman, Colonel Wyld (in the course of a speech in which he gave the Club's war casualty list as 14 members killed or died of wounds, two dead on active service and four caddies and one groundsman killed in action) had reported that the BWAC had requested the club to grow as much hay as possible. All the spare land had been treated with fertiliser and it was hoped to raise a large crop. The club was also helping the local farmers with labour. A request from the camp had been received for ground on which the cadets could practise and take exercise. Colonel Wyld undertook to select ground 'by Shand's house'. Francis Shand was the owner of The

Little House behind the 6th tee where Liz and Phil Stephens and their family now live.

It must always have been in the minds of the directors, certainly in Mr Morten's, that if the war lasted long enough they would receive such a demand from the BWAC and they were prepared to help in every possible way. Mr Morten explained to the meeting where the land might be obtained without interfering with the playing of golf and undertook to assist and provide the necessary horses. He pointed out that 37 acres of the club's land had already been taken for the use of Denham Camp. The BWAC seemed to have forgotten this in allotting the acreage. Moreover expert opinion had been obtained in 1917 as to the best use to which the land could be put. It was said to be quite useless for ploughing up and growing crops, so the land had been treated with fertiliser in the hope of a good crop of hay.

It was decided at the special meeting that these facts should be put before Mr Newton, the executive officer of the BWAC. Mr Haldane Porter and Mr Morten agreed to go to Aylesbury to see Mr Newton next day. There they pointed out that it was the BWAC's own experts who had condemned the land and this was why the club had concentrated on producing hay instead. They added that they had only one horse and no implements.

Mr Newton listened and agreed to come to look at the course himself and to examine one or two alternatives which the club put forward, such as grazing sheep.

Towards the end of February 1918 Mr Morten told the committee that work had already started beside the 3rd hole, which was then a dog-leg, and after that would move to the meadow below the stables and alongside the railway. He added that Mr Kinross, chairman of the BWAC, had been over the course with the idea of putting 500 of his own sheep on it. Mr Morten was authorised to make the best deal he could with Mr Kinross. The committee had already given permission for cadets at the camp to use the land beside the 14th for recreation.

Meanwhile the election of members went on and a new rule was instituted requiring the application for membership to state the nationality and origin of the candidate. This was prompted by a candidate bearing the fine old English name of Pratt who 'was not of Allied Nationality'. One wonders what problems might have faced Boris Karloff, whose real name was Pratt.

Relations with government departments were mixed at this time. The Air Board resolutely refused to pay for a horse hay rake damaged somehow by an aeroplane but the Ministry of Pensions wrote asking the club to employ sailors and soldiers suffering from disabilities which would be helped by work in the open air. This the committee was glad to do. The secretary attended a meeting of club secretaries in London where there was much talk of a possible luxury tax on food served in clubs. There was also a new Military Service Act which made the steward, Debnam, liable to call-up.

Major Tyler's return also led to a change of greenkeeper. The incumbent,

Flint, had appeared before a medical board and been put down to C2. The club decided that his case should be placed before the tribunal with a view to his being given a conditional exemption as being the only man left at Denham who knew anything about agriculture and was responsible for getting in the hay. Eventually on 22 June 1917 at the Eton Tribunal he was given conditional exemption bearing in mind that he was over 35, married with three children – and C2. He was then claimed as a special constable with the rank of sergeant, which presumably left him free to continue at Denham.

In the following March, however, the secretary brought to the committee's attention the unsatisfactory state of work on the course. In the major's opinion the greenkeeper had little or no control over the men, who came late and left early, and the general state of the course was evidence that little had been done during the winter. Flint had already had two distinct warnings from Major Tyler and the club captain but with little or no result. This was confirmed and Flint was given a month's notice. The staff of six henceforth would have H. Carter in charge. The rest of the greenkeeping staff, once 14 strong, were given a fortnight's notice.

By now the feeling that the war would not last much longer led to a return to the pre-war entrance fee of 10 guineas for those members elected after 1 January 1919. Suttons were asked if they would advise on the greens and on the contribution which the sheep were making to the course. Their representative was due on Tuesday 12 November.

But at the meeting on 10 November the committee had to accept Major Tyler's resignation. They passed a fervent vote of thanks to him, made him a life member of the club and invited him to take a vacant place on the committee. The major accepted. It was a momentous occasion. Next day there was another. The war ended.

4 Progress Resumed

I N THE first years after the First World War, Denham Golf Club had, or nearly had, its most successful player in terms of championships and tournaments won. Sir Ernest Holderness, to give him the title with which before long he was honoured for service in the Home Office, was one of the leading British amateurs in an age also graced by Roger Wethered and Cyril Tolley. He was a reserved slightly-built man to whom references in the archives are few.

After playing three years for Oxford from 1910, Holderness was elected a member of Denham in December 1913. He was already a member of Walton Heath. After the war he was among the 60-odd Denham members who resigned in 1919, mainly perhaps through finding jobs or homes in other parts of the country. The lack of competitions during the war may have helped to obscure the potential of a classical method and Holderness was the purest of amateurs, working until lunch on Saturdays and taking his holiday to play in the Amateur Championship. But it is significant that by October 1921, within two years of his resignation, he was being elected an honorary member of Denham. All that he had done so far was to win the first two of his four successive victories in the President's Putter when it was instituted in 1920. He added a fifth in 1929.

In 1922 he won the Amateur Championship at Prestwick and in 1924 he won it again at St Andrews. Though unable to take the time off to sail to the United States, he played in the first three Walker Cup matches staged in Britain. Against American sides which included Bobby Jones and Jess Sweetser, points for Great Britain and Ireland were hard to win but Holderness won his foursome with W.L. Hope at St Andrews in 1923. With Roger Wethered as his partner, he won a point in 1926, also at St Andrews, when they beat Francis Ouimet and J.P. Guilford.

Though his club was always given as Walton Heath, Holderness did not lose touch with Denham. Indeed when he could not accept an invitation from the Denham committee early in 1922 to play in the London Amateur Foursomes, the committee 'decided not to enter this year'. Three months later they were instructing the secretary to send a letter of congratulations on his first Amateur Championship.

CHURCHMAN'S CIGARETTES

SIR E. W. E. HOLDERNESS, BART.

Holderness played in the first international of any kind between Britain and America. This was the British team which played at Hoylake in 1921. Bobby Jones was in the US side. Holderness is seated extreme left at the front. The massive figure to his left is Cyril Tolley and Roger Wethered is directly behind Tolley

After the resignation in 1918, Major Tyler became an active member of the Denham committee and was one of the small sub-committee formed to find his successor. They soon came up with Major E.B. Hales, late Durham Light Infantry. This seems to have been another shrewd pick, for Major Hales held office until 1936.

His first AGM on 19 April, 1919 must have been a slightly unusual one, for it was preceded on March 30 by a committee meeting at which the chairman, Mr Haldane Porter, was asked to invite Colonel the Hon. F.S. Jackson, the famous cricketer, to be captain. Either because Colonel Jackson's other interests had made him unavailable at that time, or because a qualm of conscience was haunting the committee at their discarding of Mr Radley, an emergency committee meeting was held six days before the AGM. It was attended by the chairman, Mr Haldane Porter, Messrs Hibbert, Morten, Radley and Colonel Wyld, all of whom had been present at the previous meeting.

There is no record that the captaincy was discussed here but at the AGM the chairman paid a high tribute to the 'extremely valuable services rendered generally to the club during the three-year tenure of the responsible office of captain by Mr E.Y. Radley'. On behalf of the committee he submitted Mr Radley's name as captain during the 'Year of Victory'.

A year later Mr Radley was re-elected for a fifth year. Colonel Wyld followed him and it was not until 1922 that Colonel Jackson became captain. He was re-elected in 1923. Though he was at the same time MP for a Yorkshire constituency and Financial Secretary to the War Office, the earlier 1920s must have seemed restful indeed later when he was being shot at by female Bengalis.

For the captaincy in 1924, the committee submitted the name of J.E.T. Burrows, who must have been the next best golfer in the club after Colonel Jackson. In 1922 when the guidance of the R and A was sought about handicaps, the greens committee – it seemed to have gained an 's' since earlier days when 'green' was the traditional word referring to the whole course – decreed that the scratch score should be 76 'subject to the proviso that Colonel Jackson be put at plus one and J.E.T. Burrows at scratch'.

The war had brought the first signs that lawn tennis would not last at Denham. The two lower courts had survived but were in poor condition. One of two on what is now the putting green had apparently been kept in some sort of order by a horse. In December 1918 one of Major Hales's first jobs was to write to tennis members telling them that there was no chance of using the courts in 1919. If they wished, they could have their subscriptions returned. Or they could leave their names on the list as non-playing members.

The club decided to turn the two top courts into a putting green as soon as circumstances permitted and it was 1922 before the tennis future was considered again – at the AGM. There was a proposal that two courts by the clubhouse should be opened for members only and that a fixed sum should be charged for each set. Mr Morten said that the experience of the old tennis club had been that the site was too windy. He would rather propose that two hard courts be made on the site of those near the old tennis pavilion. The chairman, Mr Haldane Porter, said that in his experience golf and tennis did not go well together but that the matter would be put before the committee who would give it their very careful consideration.

However, another of the founders, Colonel Wyld, spoke in favour of reintroducing tennis and the committee recommended to the directors the provision of two courts, providing it did not entail any charge on the funds available for upkeep of the golf course.

They took a poll, sending out 496 cards, of which 235 were returned. For tennis 167. Against it 55. Open-minded 13. The committee then recommended that the lawn at present used as a putting green should be retained as such but, in view of the voting, they recommended to the directors that they should consider revival of tennis on the two lower courts. A decision on hard courts was deferred.

And that is the last reference to tennis in the records. Presumably it faded away in the later 1920s. Its main protagonist among the directors, Richard Morten, died in July 1930.

After the war 'provisional' soon became 'five-day member' and the unequal struggle to keep up the candidates book ended. The last entry was the 307th, though the total of members seemed to be over 400 whenever a count was made. An unexpected name among the 55 resignations in 1919 was that of Major Roger Way, youngest of the brothers, but that was probably because he was going overseas again and was making room for another full member from the waiting list. When he had been elected in July 1911 his occupation was given as working for the Agricultural Bank of Egypt but he was destined to be the member of the Way family who sold the land to the club 25 years later and indeed acted as honorary secretary for much of the Second World War.

The club continued to rely heavily on the railway after the war. In an attempt to prevent congestion on the 1st tee the committee had continuing discussions about how and when the 10th tee could be used for starting. In 1919 Colonel Jackson, in a joint appeal with Beaconsfield, approached the Great Central and Great Western on the possibility of having an additional train on week-day and Sunday mornings stopping at Denham Golf Club and Seer Green stations. The committee played their part by recommending to the directors that the general managers of both railways be elected hon. members *ex officio.*

The general managers replied courteously, thanking the club for making them hon. members and accepting, though there is no record of an extra train being provided.

The next exchanges between Denham and the railway companies began with a request asking if the 9.33 might stop at the Golf Club platform. This request does not seem to have been received as sympathetically as others, for the only comment in the minute book is 'motor from Denham to Gerrards Cross'. It began to look as if a beautiful friendship might be losing a little of its warmth.

During the 1920s a certain amount of rebuilding was done both on the course and in the clubhouse. As early as 1920 a projected match on the course between four professionals, including James Braid, had to be called off because of difficulty in finding a date.

There followed the very dry summer of 1921 which was especially severe on a course still only 10 years old and which, some might say, had been given too little time to settle down. The greens were rested and re-sown after an inspection by Messrs Carter of Raynes Park.

It was decided that a greenkeeper should be appointed to take sole charge of the greens. In what was described later as an inspired selection the job was given to the professional, J. Rowlands, who had returned to Denham in 1919 after demobilisation. Asked if he thought that he had enough experience to take it on, he said that he thought so and with Carter, the foreman, cooperating willingly, they seem to have brought a considerable improvement.

In his final speech as captain at the AGM in 1924 Colonel Jackson dwelt on the care needing to be exercised on the course and suggested that James Braid be asked to give his expert opinion. This was implemented at the next committee meeting with the new captain, Mr Burrows, in the chair. It was proposed that Mr Braid should be invited to go over the course and report to the greens committee. He should then make another visit to meet the greens committee and talk over his report. The effect on the course is recounted elsewhere, by Bob Fenning.

This meeting of the committee was a fairly momentous one, for one of the three new members elected was C.R. Fairey, who was to play a major part in the club's affairs 20 years later. It was also the first appearance on the committee of the famous architect Sir Giles Gilbert Scott, on whom the directors must have had their beady eye when the expansion of the clubhouse came under consideration.

James Braid

Following the Licensing Bill of 1921 the opening hours for the sale of intoxicating liquors had become 10am to 2.30pm and 4.30pm to 8pm on weekdays; 12 noon to 2pm and 6pm to 8 on Sundays. This seemed to cause no great hardship to anyone but did rather concentrate the mind on the inadequacy of the bar.

If one entered the clubhouse by the main door and turned right, the bar was at the end of the passage and apparently no wider than the passage. This is how Carl Chronander, the oldest playing member in 1991, remembered it. He first became a member of Denham in 1929.

Colonel Wyld laid before the committee the question of the enlargement of the bar, after which it was proposed that the enlargement should be 'gone on with'. The grammar may have been shaky but the soundness of the idea was unchallengeable. A sub-committee was formed – three representing the directors, three the committee – to examine the plans for alterations to the clubhouse.

The need for greater security was no doubt to the fore. Few golf clubs are

not vulnerable to theft and indeed golf clubs must be to housebreaking what nursery slopes are to skiing. Greater vigilance was being urged on members and did not go unrewarded. A diamond and ruby brooch was found on the club's property and the secretary was given permission to 'lodge it with Scotland Yard'.

Gifts to the club had soon started coming in again after the war. The first gift of the grandfather clock, the one presented by Mr John Mews in August 1913, still stands proudly in the dining-room alcove.

The cup given by Mr J. Clayton Hardie in April 1922 is still contested under the conditions suggested by the donor – for the best aggregate score in the monthly medals of April and May.

In 1922 the club instituted the custom of making the lady Amateur champion an honorary member while she was champion. For three of the next four years she was Joyce Wethered.

In April 1923 Colonel Wyld offered to present the club with a set of bowls but the committee declined his kind offer 'at the present time', presumably judging that life was complicated enough as it was without having bowls as well as tennis to cope with.

The possible purchase of the course by the club had been looming again with discussions involving the directors and committee. Colonel Wyld reiterated that the board of directors were anxious to buy the course and explained the position. He had been assured by Colonel Way's solicitors that there was no prospect of any further building in Collsels Wood, as there were no more suitable sites. Collsels Wood is the one between the 12th green and the 18th fairway. The discussions continued into 1924 when, after the business of the day had been completed, Colonel Wyld told the committee what progress had been made towards obtaining a 40-year lease. He asked the committee for their opinions.

Digby Cotes-Preedy KC, the Recorder of Smethwick, who had been increasingly active in the club's affairs and was to become a director in 1925, expressed the approval of the committee, but it was to be another 20 years before the ultimate aim of owning the club was achieved.

When one reads in the Sunday papers or hears of the hostile treatment of women golfers by men, or the other way round, one can marvel at the harmony between them at Denham, though Major Hales seems to have been under some emotion when replying at about this time to a letter from the lady captain.

'The Committee cannot see its way', he wrote, 'to allow the reserving of caddies for the whole day, as suggested. If ladies *will* engage caddies for the whole day, though playing only one round, this will become the caddies' preference.' To the caddies, walking half the distance for the same money must have seemed good economics.

At about this time a body called the Caddies Scout Camp Troop wrote to the club for information. There was no messing about. The Committee passed it straight on to the Chief Scout himself for him to supply the required information.

For the captaincy in 1925 the committee nominated Thomas McMeekin, the fourth of the six surviving founders to have become captain. This left Colonel Way, who was not a golfer and as the landlord was in a special position, and Mr Morten.

At the end of his year in office Mr McMeekin reflected on the 'wonderful progress' made by the club despite the war, in just 15 years. He said that the past year had been noteworthy for two events, the further bunkering of the course by James Braid and the granting of the 40-year extension of the lease by Colonel Way.

Mr McMeekin paid the usual tributes to the committee and directors, to the greenkeeper and his staff and to the clubhouse staff. But he went further than this. He also gave a plug to the golf club, which was reported in the *Middlesex Advertiser* and other local papers, and must have been a very fair piece of public relations in that day and age:

> Mr McMeekin emphasised clearly how greatly a club such as this benefited the district in general, apart from its own members. Since its institution in 1911 a sum of no less than £30,000 had been paid to its employees, apart from the very considerable amount earned by caddies. All this tended to solve the all-important problem of unemployment. The revenue claimed large sums in taxes, whilst the local Union enjoyed a large addition to the poor rate. Amongst those who also benefited were the local tradesmen who supplied the Club and carried out the repairs to the Club house, cottages etc. Were these to be tabulated the total expenditure would include some astonishing figures.

5 The Twenties

OR THE first 15 years in the life of Denham Golf Club Mr W. Haldane Porter was in the forefront of its affairs. Knighted in 1926 and having retired from the Home Office, Sir William moved to Dublin and at 63 became assistant managing director of Guinness. His place at Denham was largely taken by a fellow KC, and his next door neighbour in Gerrards Cross, Digby Cotes-Preedy. Colonel Wyld was the chairman of the company and Sir Giles Gilbert Scott was increasingly active.

The General Strike of May 1926 extended the gap between committee meetings to seven weeks but there is no record of its causing any inconvenience otherwise. In July 1926 Colonel Way was being thanked for yet another gift to the club, this time a cup to be played for at an Open meeting in the autumn.

Mr J.C. Hibbert, another of the seven founders and the first captain of the club, presented a picture of himself shortly before he moved to Essex. The hon. treasurer, J.S. Skidmore, who had done that job since the beginning, resigned as he too was leaving the district. He was replaced by Major T. South, his successor as manager of Barclay's Bank, Uxbridge.

At the AGM of 1927 the captain, Mr Cotes-Preedy, spoke with regret of the resignation from the committee of Mr McMeekin. The incoming captain was Mr H.G. Muskett, 'well known in legal circles and resident in Gerrards Cross', as the *Bucks Advertiser* put it. He was destined to have his year in office extended to two years, partly because of a period of ill health in his first year and partly, too, perhaps because he was needed to command the manning of the ramparts against Oswald Mosley which came early in his second year.

Otherwise, with the General Strike out of the way, domestic affairs dominated, such as the admission of ladies to the bar, the potholes in Tilehouse Lane, the alterations to the course – and more worming. The worms, it seems, were fighting back.

At the end of 1926 the secretary reported 36 resignations and 21 vacancies for full members. This probably reflects both the modest expense of joining clubs in this area and yet the shortage of young men and women who could afford it.

The club matches for 1927 were listed as being against the Jokers, Air

Ministry, Home Office, Bar Golfing Society, House of Commons G.S., Household Brigade and the Old Etonians. One other which was being mooted and which was to prove as productive a source of new members and good golfers as any, was against Cambridge University.

The Denham Ladies seemed to have a much closer relationship with the Bucks Ladies than the men did with the BB and O who seemed to be suspected of threatening the club's independence and individuality. Indeed in 1927 the Bucks Ladies played their Challenge Cup meeting and a county match at Denham. Miss Cecil Leitch, one of the best British lady golfers of the day, became an honorary member. Her matches with Joyce Wethered had led to a stirring era in ladies golf and in 1926 she had won the British Ladies Championship for the third time. She was subsequently to present the club with a spectacular bronze model, not over-dressed, which is contested annually in a competition for both men and women.

In one other respect the thinking of the lady members advanced ahead of the men's. A letter from the ladies suggesting that there should be club colours met with a guarded reply to the effect that there was no objection, 'provided that the club be not liable to pay any of the expenditure incurred'.

The special arrangements made during the war for the personnel of local Service installations to play at Denham were largely retained for, amongst others, the RAF stations at Uxbridge, Ruislip and Northolt.

One sign of the times in 1929 was the query from the then Mr C.R. Fairey, the aircraft manufacturer, regarding the use of steel-shafted clubs in competitions. The secretary was instructed by the committee to write to him regretting that his suggestion 'which is contrary to the Rules of St Andrews' could not be adopted. The steel shaft was not legitimised until 1930.

Another example of changing times came with Colonel Wyld's statement in June 1927

Joyce Wethered and Cecil Leitch, early 1920s

that the question of installing electric light was being considered by the directors. He hoped that this would be favourably entertained by the committee, which it was. In the 1920s there were still many villages and farms within 20 odd miles of London relying on oil lamps.

Increasing thought was being given to young golfers. A junior competition in the Christmas holidays was organised by a special sub-committee headed by the captain, Mr Muskett. The sons and daughters of members and their friends were allowed to play at weekends starting after 4pm and paying a green fee of 1s 6d ($7\frac{1}{2}$p) per round.

With the average age of members being so much higher than it is now, there was a far greater demand for caddies in those pre-trolley days and the committee were in agreement that Wyatt, the caddie-master, needed more help on Sundays.

A notable resignation in 1929 was that of Sir Francis Lacey who had been secretary of MCC for 28 years before his retirement in 1926 aged 67. He was credited with having tightened the administration at Lord's, though not to the extent of ending the traditional 'golf-break' there every spring. He had become a member of Denham in 1912 on a director's nomination of Mr McMeekin. His assistant-secretary at Lord's, A. Cornwall Legh, had been elected on Commander Tarleton's nomination in 1911 but had not survived the war.

The Tarleton Cup continued to flourish, though to give it initial impetus the first two rounds in 1930 were played on a Sunday in March.

The Tarleton Cup

That year there was the rare occurrence of a contest for the two vacant places on the committee and the even rarer publication of the votes which were cast. F.G.M. Chancellor, a member since 1911 and the architect of recent rebuilding of the clubhouse, polled 31 votes; Gilbert Heron, also a pre-war member, 29; and C.R. Fairey, a member for two years, 4. It must have been an entirely predictable result and there is no evidence of any acrimony or embarrassment but, in the light of their later contributions, it was lucky for the golf club that the future Sir Richard Fairey, and his seconder, Turberville Smith, were not discouraged.

Otherwise Denham Golf Club could not be said to be parochial. In 1928 Senor Catone N. Nicoreanu, the Chilean consul in Brighton, was elected to temporary full membership at a fee of 6 guineas. In 1929 the South African cricket team touring England were made honorary members for the summer; and in 1930 the fixtures included a match against the agents-general of the Empire.

For some years there had in effect been no professional at Denham, for Rowlands' success as a greenkeeper had left him no time for anything else. But on his death in 1929 the greenkeeping could be safely left to Carter and his staff and a new professional, A.J. Miles, was appointed. The committee recommended that he should compete in the Open Championship of 1930 which was to be held at Hoylake and which proved a historic event. It was the second leg of Bobby Jones's unique 'grand slam'. He had already won the Amateur Championship at St Andrews that summer and he went home to win the US Open and finally the US Amateur.

Early in 1930 the highly successful captaincy of Sir Giles Gilbert Scott was coming to an end and the committee unanimously nominated O.E. Coles to succeed him. However, there must have been some profound rethinking, for a month later they unanimously nominated Lieut. Colonel B.I. Way DSO for the job. It may be that Mr Coles was unable to accept but more likely, one would imagine, they suddenly realised that this might be their last chance to show their appreciation of Colonel Way's boundless generosity. At the AGM Sir Giles listed the latest examples of this as a new reaper, half the cost of a new motor mower, wood and the gravel and labour for paths round the clubhouse.

As Colonel Way was not a golfer, the committee gave him Sir Giles as vice-captain.

The fact that Colonel Way did not play golf may have been a factor in not making him captain in the early days. It may have been thought by some, and by the colonel himself, that as the club's landlord he was disqualified from taking up the captaincy. Moreover, he was a great traveller – he was in Demerara when the invitation to become captain reached him only two days before the AGM. But any complications arising out of his dual roles must have disappeared with the granting of the 40-year lease and, with Sir Giles Scott in close support, he embarked on a 'wonderfully smooth' year which ended with his being succeeded by an old friend, Mr R.M. Rowley-Morris.

Early in the colonel's year of office he found himself with the sad task of paying tributes to the third of his fellow-founders to die, Richard Morten, who in war and peace-time had made divers contributions to the club's development. In his speech as the retiring captain on 18 April 1931 Colonel Way looked back over nearly 21 years, remembering others who had played major parts in the club's success.

He mentioned Rowlands, the professional-turned-greenkeeper; the steward and stewardess, Mr and Mrs Debnam, who had come to the club on the same day in 1912 that the Denham Golf Club Halt was opened; R. Wyatt, the caddiemaster, and H. Stiles who remained of the original staff; Charlie Stone who arrived only six months later. In the clubhouse Hilda Lawrence had played an invaluable part since 1915.

There was nothing to suggest that Colonel Way's health was failing, indeed he served on the house committee after he stepped down as captain. He was present at several meetings of the general committee in that summer of 1931 and at one in the following May. But, on 1 October 1932, a telegram arrived at Denham from Pietermaritzburg with the news that he had died there that day.

Telegrams were sent to his two brothers, Major Gerald Way in Egypt and Major Roger Way in Pietermaritzburg:

'We all deeply sympathise with you and your family in your sad bereavement. We have all lost an old and valued friend.'

The Course in 1925

View from the 4th tee

Approaching the 17th green

6 In Search of Members

THE 1930s were difficult years for many reasons. The 1929 summer had been very dry and the watering systems of the day could not do much about it. Moreover the depression did not end with the slump of 1931 and the formation of a National Government. Public spending was severely cut. Work on new roads was stopped. Economies abounded in what is now called the leisure industry and West End theatres advertised two seats for the price of one. Golf clubs did not escape.

There seem to be two differences between a depression in the 1930s and those of today. In the later 1930s if petrol went up a penny, it still only cost the equivalent of 8p a gallon. Yet now, when most golf clubs, and indeed other sporting clubs such as MCC, have long waiting lists, they were then trying to attract new membership.

During Mr Rowley-Morris's year of captaincy, 1931, he foresaw some 50 vacancies for full members by the end of it and suggested that the committee should recommend to the directors an increase in lady members from 75 to 100. In 1932 the number of full members who resigned was 53, eight others had died; 16 five-day members had resigned, one had died. The Christmas Fund for the staff was a barometer – at £218 it was down £8 on the previous year. In his speech at the AGM as the retiring captain, Mr Rowley-Morris said that the committee and directors hoped that members would bring the club to the notice of their friends with a view to becoming members of it.

The *Buckinghamshire Advertiser* recorded that Mr Rowley Morris had finished his year in office with a flourish. At the 15th (then a bogey 5), he holed from 30 yards for a 3. On the 16th tee the caddy of one of his opponents said: 'We can't play against that, sir. I suppose you'll do this in one.' Which Mr Rowley-Morris did.

In a mixed foursome some 40 years later Mrs Joan Elliot did something similar at the preceding holes. She holed with a 4-wood at the 13th from 150 yards and when she took out the same club at the 14th for a shot of the same length, it was frivolously suggested that she might repeat her former feat. But this time she only hit the flag.

In 1932 the Committee included, for the first time, Walter Henderson whose *Tatler* caricature in the bar faithfully portrays his vigorous swing. He was captain in 1936, 23 years before his son John. *The Tatler* caricatures were bought by the captains of 1932 and 1933, G.H. Jennings and H.R. Rudd, and given to the club.

H.R. Rudd

It was generally agreed that the arrival of A.J. Miles as professional had brought about an improvement in the golf of the members. He was still playing in some tournaments and in 1932 the committee wished him luck and sent him off to Sandwich to play in the Open at Prince's with £10 towards his expenses. But when it came to finding the £125 to £150 for building a shelter by the 1st tee, they drew back.

It was decided to put up a list in the club house inviting members to subscribe towards the cost. It was agreed that a shelter would be a boon and a blessing to all on those winter mornings when the north-east wind blew unresisted across the airfield and it would come in useful on hot summer days when refreshments were needed after nine holes. But the committee 'did not feel justified at the present time in recommending the expenditure to the Directors'. It was decided to ascertain if members would be prepared to defray the cost by individual subscriptions. Only two members did and the appeal was dropped.

In February 1934, however, Mr C.R. Fairey came on the scene, not for the last time, and his offer to provide the club with a shelter was gratefully accepted. The committee said that they would look forward to seeing the plans which he proposed to present for their approval. They suggested that 'Mr Fairey or his architect might perhaps meet Sir Giles Scott here.'

By May 1934 the site for the shelter had been definitely fixed and pegged out. Members of the committee were asked to inspect the site that day, as work was to start almost immediately. By early July Mr Fairey, with Mrs Fairey, was being invited to come and hand over the shelter to the club at a small opening ceremony.

At the AGM on 1 April 1933, Mr Jennings, the retiring captain, was accorded the usual vote of thanks by Mr Cotes-Preedy, who was a rare hand at such courtesies. He must have excelled himself with this one, for the *Buckinghamshire Advertiser* referred to 'a short and excellent speech which included certain humorous passages'. Mr Jennings, no less to the point, said that his successor, Mr H.R. Rudd, needed no introduction, as every one knew his cheery nature and, 'whilst he is a good golfer, he has, better still, the interest of the Club at heart'.

Mr Rudd did not let anyone down and, as he had been absent on business in America for part of the year, he was re-elected for a second year. He rounded off his first year in style, for the regular committee meeting in February took place, not in the clubhouse, but at 3 St James's Street, SW1. Mr Rudd, of course, was the Rudd of Berry Bros and Rudd and on their premises 'the Committee and Secretary were most

hospitably entertained to dinner by the Captain of the Club.'

Relations with the ladies became more cordial than ever as they presented the club with the prizes for the men's Autumn Meeting. The club committee responded by deciding that the lady captain should be coopted on to the house committee *ex officio*.

There was some unease at this time about the state of the course and a small but high-powered sub-committee was appointed to consult Harry Colt, the original architect who in the early archives had only once been mentioned – and then only as the recipient of a small payment some time after the course was open. Much of the subsequent report was acted upon in the autumn of 1935.

One of the Rudd salvers

One action recommended was the planting of poplars and firs to form a copse betweeen the 2nd fairway and the road. The exposure of cars and pedestrians in Tilehouse Lane to a sliced drive from the second tee had been worrying the committee for some time and Mr Oakle and Mr Henderson had recently increased the third party insurance.

The good luck which the club had enjoyed with its staff in various vitally important places began to run out in 1933 with the resignation of the steward and stewardess through Mrs Debnam's ill health. They had given 21 years' service and were much missed, especially as it was some years before the positions were filled satisfactorily. Hilda Lawrence, a pillar of the clubhouse for $17\frac{1}{2}$ years, resigned at the same time. A fund for her and the Debnams jointly was launched.

Carter, the foreman of the earlier days, who had become a highly successful head greenkeeper, was absent for several months with a serious illness and in 1937 had to retire.

Colonel Hales, the secretary, also had to retire through failing health in 1936. He was made an honorary life member but died in the following year. The honorary treasurer of the last 10 years, Major South, also retired, as he was leaving the district.

This upheaval meant that Walter Henderson's year of captaincy was the opposite of a rest cure but order seems to have been restored by the time he handed over to Mr C.T. Carr, later Sir Cecil, in March 1937. Major R.J. Boothby arrived as secretary. After some misfires a new steward and stewardess were installed in J.A. Fulford and his sister Mrs Mason.

The membership increased, helped by a suspension of the entrance fee which Mr Carr stressed would not be allowed to lower the standard of the membership. There had been no obvious evidence of this so far. Indeed the club had acquired a new honorary life member in HRH Prince Arthur of Connaught, grandson of Queen Victoria and first cousin of King George V who had died in the previous January. Prince Arthur was a popular and informal figure who died in 1938, before both his father and his only son.

A sentence in Mr Henderson's address is a reminder that the front of the clubhouse was, as late as 1937, not where one would expect to find it now.

'It is proposed', he said, 'to make the old tennis courts in front of the clubhouse into an up-to-date putting course.'

The committee had had to withstand more than one attempt to divert the club from its *raison d'etre*. Having shaken off the tennis section, they gave a firm no to a member who suggested that the putting green might be used for croquet and they fended off a suggestion that it might be turned into a bowling green, saying that this would not be considered unless there was a sufficient demand from members. However, when the game suggested was bridge, with its obvious attraction on days when the weather made golf a penance, they lent a sympathetic ear and asked Colonel Wyld to form a sub-committee to deal with the matter.

At this time Colonel Wyld seems to have been heavily involved elsewhere, whether or not with the board of Fortnum and Mason is not stated. He was also at the heart of improvements being planned for the course and Mr Rudd had to tell the members of the committee that he was unable to show them Mr Colt's report as it had not been returned by Colonel Wyld in time for the meeting. He said that in the near future Mr Cotes-Preedy, Sir Giles Scott and Mr Rudd himself, the special sub-committee appointed to consider the report, would be on holiday together at Brancaster where they would discuss the report at their leisure and formulate their suggestions.

Bridge, therefore, seems to have been lost in the brouhaha, though there was no obvious objection to it. But all must have ended happily, for in 1937 there came a suggestion that during the winter a bridge afternoon should be instituted. The committee said that if found feasible, it had their support.

Hard times they may have been but there was no shortage of votes of thanks to members who had undertaken specific jobs. Mr and Mrs A.P. Saunders were thanked for all the work they had done towards making the improvements in the men's and ladies' changing-rooms such a success; Captain O.D. Freeman was thanked for installing a complete new hot-water

heating system in the caddies' shelter at his own expense; and there seemed to be few meetings at which Sir Giles Gilbert Scott was not being thanked for something or other.

Though a director since 1927, Sir Giles was temporarily off the committee when he proposed a screen for the dining hall and sent a sketch of it. The committee immediately agreed that it should be bought 'under the advice of Sir Giles'. When the names of winners of the Muskett Gold Medal filled the gold bars on it, it was proposed that a name-board, 'style and position to be recommended by Sir Giles', be bought and erected showing the names of previous winners. When improvements on the course were needed, the small sub-committee which was asked to talk to the original architect included Sir Giles.

He was back on the committee in 1938 when alterations to the club's premises were being discussed and he volunteered that he had further suggestions in mind regarding the kitchens. It is an awesome thought that the mind which conjured up Liverpool Cathedral and the War Memorial Chapel at Charterhouse was now being brought to bear on the kitchens of Denham Golf Club.

A worthy move during Mr Henderson's year of captaincy in 1936 had been the introduction of juvenile membership, open to the sons and daughters of members up to the age of 18 at an annual subscription of 3 guineas without entrance fee.

Sir Giles Scott in later years, about to tee off at Hoylake's 1st hole in the early 1950s

'Such members to be allowed to play as Five-Day Members but to give way both on the tee and through the green. They are not entitled to attend or vote at meetings.'

Mr Henderson had also been responsible for a useful ruling about dogs, born of a query in the suggestion book about the standing of dogs on the course. It was decided – 'as a tentative measure' – to allow dogs on the course on a lead. If, however, this was not strictly observed, the whole question would be reconsidered. They were not allowed in the clubhouse.

In 1937 the question of £1 green fees for visitors on Sundays and 6s on week-days, unaccompanied by a member, was discussed by the committee. It was generally agreed that they were too high but no decision was reached about amending them in view of the possible revision of the scale of green fees. If these charges seemed too high, the same could scarcely be said of the price of drinks, which had just been changed as follows:

One small glass of port came down from 1s to 9d
One small glass of kummel came down from 1s 6d to 1s
One small glass of whisky went up 8d to 9d
One small glass of gin went up 8d to 9d

After the death of Colonel B.I. Way in South Africa in October 1932 his brother, Major Gerald Way DSO, became the landlord of Denham Golf Club. In 1934 he was elected to the committee and served until his death in June 1938. The loss of their landlord, a director of the club and one of their own number passed unmentioned in the minutes of the committee, no doubt because of the tragic nature of his death.

In April 1939, on the recommendation of the directors, it was resolved that Mr Lewis B.R. Way, elder son of Major Roger Way be elected an honorary life member of the club. His father had recently become a non-playing member and it was presumably intended that Lewis Way would become the club's landlord and, it may be, the member of the family who would sooner or later be negotiating the sale of the land.

The outbreak of the Second World War changed all that. Lewis Way joined the RAF, the secretary Major Boothby was soon back in the Army and within a few days Major Roger Way, now the landlord, became the honorary secretary.

7 Landlord in Waiting

FOR MUCH of the between-wars period Major Roger Way had had little to do with Denham Golf Club. For 12 years he was living in South Africa with his family.

In 1915 Lieutenant Roger Way had married Brenda Lathbury, youngest of the five daughters of the late rector of Denham. It was intended to be a very quiet wedding because the bride's father had died only recently but the local papers brushed that aside with a column or more. One had the compelling headline: 'Interesting Nuptials at Denham'. The then Lieutenant Way, already twice wounded, was serving in the North Staffordshire Regiment, in which his elder brother Ben commanded the 4th Battalion.

In 1922 Major and Mrs Roger Way, with their two small sons, arrived in Pietermaritzburg. He had selected the capital of Natal for their home after a careful reconnaissance. He was described in a local paper as a retired soldier with shell shock.

However, the major soon made an impact on the somewhat turgid public life of Natal. His performance in the Victoria League's 1923 production of *The Importance of being Earnest* led one dramatic critic to comment: 'Major R.H. Way is evidently a man of many parts. One had known him as a very fluent speaker with a most telling delivery but he proved that he is a sufficiently good actor to make a tiny part show up.'

In April 1924 he was organising secretary of the Maritzburg Gala and Shopping Week. Of his 'splendid work' in this role the editorial in the *Natal Witness* said 'Here is a very observant and much travelled man who has come amongst us, who thinks that we have a beautiful city which should be widely advertised as offering advantages from every point of view. His great enthusiasm . . . is causing him to put an amount of energy into his work which could not be forced.'

He threw himself into advertising Maritzburg in that year's Empire Exhibition at Wembley. He was an indefatigable worker for Toc H and for the Zwarthof Valley Ratepayers' Association. He took an active part in the campaigns for better roads, better lighting and water-borne sewage.

Yet he and his wife never lost touch with life in South Buckinghamshire, as is evident from the scrapbook which she painstakingly maintained. They went home in the summer of 1926 and were present at Major Gerald Way's wedding in Gerrards Cross to a widow from Farnborough. In the following year his brother Ben came out to Maritzburg and stayed with them on his way to what the papers called 'a little game shooting'.

In 1929 Roger Way was persuaded to stand as a Reform candidate in a by-election for a vacancy in the city council. Once he had decided that he could do more from within the council, he addressed himself to the hustings with characteristic energy and won with 1,055 to Mr T.G. Jones's 468. The loser said that he was overwhelmed by Major Way's success. 'I am sport enough', he said, 'to congratulate him on his splendid victory. It is the biggest hiding I have had in the many elections I have taken part in.'

For two years the major seems to have kept the council on its toes but in 1931 when he had steered through his own proposals for relief work and promoted other good causes, he refused to offer himself for re-election, saying that he was sure the other candidate would do his best for Ward II and the city in general.

In 1932 his brother, Colonel Benjamin Irby Way, came to stay with him again, this time on his way back from a fishing trip on the Zambesi, but he had contracted a severe attack of malaria there. He died in Grey's Hospital, Maritzburg – in the country where he had first joined the North Staffordshire Regiment in 1890.

By the end of the Roger Ways' stay in South Africa his two sons were showing sporting ability which the major stoutly upheld by finishing second in that most gruelling of events, the fathers' race. He was then 50. With the superbly situated Hilton College only just outside Maritzburg, Michaelhouse at no great distance and Maritzburg College in the city, there was no shortage of good schools but Major and Mrs Way had decided that the time had come to return home.

His brother Gerald was now the landlord of the golf club and on the committee and remained so until the grievous day in June 1938 when he died.

The devotion of the Way family to Denham and its people weighed so heavily on Major Gerald Way DSO that when he was due to move to Suffolk, he found that he could not face it. He drove his wife to Suffolk and returned to the house in Bulstrode Way, Gerrards Cross, where he had been living since the sale of Denham Place in the early 1920s. He spent the night there and saw the last pieces of furniture out of the house.

Next morning he set off, apparently for Suffolk, but stopped in Hollybush Lane, Tatling End, which was still part of the Way land. There he met one of his gamekeepers and talked to him for a few minutes about birds before asking if he might borrow his gun. He then drove 100 yards back up the lane and shot himself. He was 63 and, it was said, 'a gentleman loved and respected by all who knew him'.

At the inquest Roger Way said that there was no good reason why his brother should take his life but he had noticed that he had not seemed himself in the last month and had been worried that he had not yet been able to sell the house in Bulstrode Way.

Roger Way was soon taking over many of the duties previously carried out by his brothers and those of their sister who had died in 1931. He was patron of the living of Denham and in 1939 persuaded a cousin, the Rev. Charles Way, to move from Eccleshall in Staffordshire to the rectory at Denham, where, of course, Mrs Roger Way had spent her childhood.

Their elder son, Lewis, had rowed bow in the Maiden Erlegh boat and was now at London University but at Stowe, his younger brother, Tony, was one of a pair of half-backs outstanding in any era of schools rugby football. Their most memorable victory was the 67–0 win over Radley.

A.G. Way, the scrum-half, was said in *The Times* to be larger than many of the forwards on the field but he formed a partnership with his stand-off half, Peter Hastings, which was the decisive factor throughout Stowe's unbeaten progress in that season of 1938–9.

Peter Hastings-Bass, as he became later to meet the provisions of Sir William Bass's will, was an exceptional athlete and games player, the more effective for being strongly built for his years. He was one of the best young quarter-milers in the country and, while in the Welsh Guards, played rugby for England in seven war-time Services internationals. He was training racehorses successfully, some for the Queen, when he died in 1964 aged 43. His son, William, now Lord Huntingdon, is similarly engaged in the 1990s.

The Stowe pair were picked for the England Schoolboys in the annual New Year match at Richmond run by Richmond and the London Scottish and though Way was handicapped by an injury suffered in the first half, the Scottish boys were disposed of 13–6.

That was at the start of 1939. By the end of it Tony Way was at Sandhurst and about to be commissioned. He was made an honorary life member of Denham in 1946 and now lives in Perthshire. Lewis Way was in the RAF training to be a fighter pilot – he was twice shot down in the Battle of Britain. Major Roger Way was finding an outlet for his energy and organisational skill in the demanding war-time job of honorary secretary of Denham Golf Club.

8 War and Requisition

IN FEBRUARY 1939 Mr C.R. Fairey succeeded Major Gilbert Heron as captain. It was appreciated that he might not be able to find the time to do the job properly and the committee had agreed that if he could not accept, a sub-committee comprising Major Heron, Sir Giles Gilbert Scott and Mr Rudd should recommend someone else for the office. One of the considerations in the months after Munich was, of course, the possibility of war, which would affect an aircraft manufacturer more than most.

However, Mr Fairey did accept, though at the AGM he said that if he could not give as much time to his duties as captain as he would like, he hoped that members would understand that it was not due to any lack of interest.

His fears were well founded. After presiding over two committee meetings in the spring of 1939 he was prevented both by pressure of work and ill health from attending another. Major Heron acted for him until the spring of 1940 before handing over to Anthony Pickford. It was agreed that Mr Fairey would be nominated again in easier times.

These were certainly difficult times for a golf club. By the spring of 1940 the resignations exceeded 100. Another 72 had changed grade. The war was only three weeks old when the committee ruled that 'any member who is engaged on active service shall be considered as an Honorary Member of the Club for the duration of the War.' (Similar courtesies were, of course, extended throughout the country. The writer of this history was made an honorary member of the Royal and Ancient while bringing his dubious military expertise to bear on the task of fortifying St Andrews.)

The swift introduction of petrol coupons, which at the basic rate allowed the motorist only about 150 miles a month, must have accounted for many resignations and though Denham's railway halt came into its own again, it could do little for those with a cross-country journey to make. As the black-out became ever earlier that autumn, the dining room became less usable and was soon to be put out of action for five years. The committee wrestled unendingly with the problem of charging green fees and subscriptions which were fair to everyone but would also provide a sum which would help to keep the club alive.

There was an acute shortage of staff both on the course and in the

'Red Cross Golf Match, 'Denham, 14th July 1940

Left to Right: A.J. Miles, A.F.I. Pickford (Capt. Denham Club), Henry Cotton,
Sandy Herd, W.T. Cox, Major Way (Hon. Secretary).

clubhouse. Wyatt, the long-serving caddie-master, was in poor health. The professional, A.J. Miles, and the steward and stewardess, Mr and Mrs Brayley, put their hands to jobs far removed from those for which they were intended. As was later revealed at the AGM, Mr Miles had most willingly accepted a reduction in pay. Mr and Mrs Brayley had spontaneously offered one. Charlie Stone, and the three others of the greenkeeping staff left, had kept the course in a condition which visitors envied. One of the oldest members of the staff, H. Styles, had 'taken on many new duties in the most cheerful and willing manner'.

The efforts of all concerned to keep the course and club going was made harder by the deaths of three stalwarts. The biggest shock, in the autumn of 1941, was that of Major Gilbert Heron, who had been in the forefront of the club's administration since war broke out. A solicitor, he had been a member since 1912.

H. Carter, for so long a pillar of the greenkeeping staff, died in the following spring. Later in 1942 Digby Cotes-Preedy was being mourned.

His Honour Judge Cotes-Preedy, as he had been known since just before the war, was so hard to replace, despite his long illness, that Major Way, who had been trying to keep committee meetings to a minimum because of increasing transport difficulties, called an extra meeting to draft a suitable letter of sympathy and consider the implications of Mr Cotes-Preedy's death. For more than ten years he had been a most active director and member of committees. The judge's son, Pat Cotes-Preedy, though one of the leading members of the Bar in Nottingham, was still often to be seen at Denham until his death in 1990.

For the rest of the war and through the negotiations which led up to the momentous purchase of the club from its honorary secretary, Major Roger Way, the captain of the club was Mr Turberville Smith, the Uxbridge solicitor. Colonel Wyld, the last of the seven founders to be still active, seldom missed a meeting. Nor did Mr R.B. Templeton, one of the best golfers in the club with a handicap of three, and nor did Mr W. Eves, Fleet Paymaster and a member since 1918.

Mr Eves was a fine example of the old adage, 'Cometh the Hour, Cometh the Man'. He was clearly a wizard at requisition – or, to be exact, at minimising the more painful effects of it.

At the end of May 1941 the then captain, Mr Pickford, spoke with reasonable confidence of the future while thanking those members who had contributed £600 to the club with no other promise than that it should be maintained to the end of the year. He had handed over to Mr Turberville Smith with the jovial comment that it showed great confidence in the legal profession that for two years running the captain should be drawn from their ranks. In the event, Mr Turberville Smith's term as captain was to be extended to five years.

Already there had been a reference to Mrs Brayley's feat in cooking for some 50 to 60 RAF personnel during the week and at weekends providing 40 members with really excellent lunches. But negotiations with the RAF were still going on.

The art of being requisitioned without tears seems to lie in building up such warm personal relations that the requisitioner on the ground will fight your battle against higher authority for you. He will also keep the place tidy – easier then, perhaps, when vandalism had not reached the high standards of hooliganism of today – get you a useful rent and at the end of it a healthy compensation. Bob Fenning reveals the effect of the RAF occupation of the course and buildings at Denham elsewhere.

Thus at the AGM Mr Turberville Smith had been able to report that the financial position of the club had hardly deteriorated at all in the past year.

In 1941 the foundations of a Denham Artisans Club had been laid. Early in 1943 the hon. secretary told the committee that he had received an application from six residents of Higher Denham – the village which grew up between the wars on the other side of the railway by the halt – to join the club under artisan terms. The committee decided that any resident in the parish of Denham should be eligible to join a Denham Artisan Golfing Association to be promoted by the club under such rules and regulations as might be decided later.

At the committee meeting in May 1943 Major Way reported on the progress of the association and it was agreed that a circular letter signed by the chairman, Colonel Wyld, should be sent to all members.

In June Mr Turberville Smith told of the meeting which he and Major Way had had with representatives of the association. The committee formally approved of the membership rules as prepared. Though this was the summer when the possible purchase of the club from Major Way was exercising the mind of most members, the drafting of the rules for an artisans club by the greens committee seems to have progressed to the satisfaction of all.

Major Way, who lived at Badminton House in Marsham Way, Gerrards Cross, at the time, must have been working long hours as hon. secretary, but as landlord he reduced the rent which was due to him from the club. He allowed himself a whimsical comment in the minutes on his dual role:

'It was duly proposed and seconded that the Hon. Secretary be instructed to write to Major R. Way, requesting him not to renew his Temporary Membership, on the grounds that he had informed the Captain that it was an "imposition" that he should be asked to pay his subscription!'

While the sale and purchase of the club were still uncertain, the AGM of 1943 was delayed and it was not until 14 August that the historic meeting took place. In the first part of it Mr Turberville Smith reported that the club had had a successful year both from the social and golfing point of view. It had raised £346 for the *Daily Sketch* Comforts Fund. He thanked all who had helped to achieve this despite shortages and many other frustrations.

The hon. secretary then addressed the meeting and said that he had taken it on himself to ask that there should be no change in the committee at this time. It would, he said, make his task very much easier to have the backing of a captain and committee who were fully cognizant of all the affairs of the club. This was agreed.

Mr Turberville Smith then opened the second part of the meeting. Speaking as chairman of the special committee set up when Major Way made known his intention to sell the freehold of the club, he said that they had all considered the £13,000 asked as being a very reasonable figure for the course and land. It included all buildings except Oakleigh, later John Sheridan's house, which Major Way wanted for his son Lewis to live in after the war.

Oakleigh

The committee considered that it needed to raise £17,000 altogether but the fund set up had been disappointing, amounting to barely a quarter of this. Unless the £17,000 was forthcoming, said Mr Turberville Smith, it would be good-bye to the club they all loved so much. He then called on Jack Moir who, he said, was fully qualified to go into the accounts for the pre-war period, and to give his carefully worked-out estimate of future expenditure in the post-war period.

This Mr Moir did with gusto. When he sat down, he was given a standing ovation by the 30-odd members present. Somebody suggested that if the club did not buy the property, there would be many people ready to do so. Major Way promptly said that he was not prepared to sell it to anyone else at the same price.

The last spark of doubt had been dowsed. It was formally proposed and seconded that Major Way's offer to sell the freehold for £13,000 should be accepted. This was carried unanimously.

The £4,000 already subscribed was returned and the club set about raising the money by debentures. But fund-raising in 1943 and 1944 was at its nadir and there was still a short-fall. A cable was sent to Sir Richard Fairey who was in America. He came up with £2,500. The final £1,000 was subscribed, in the quixotic tradition of his family – by the vendor, Major Roger Way.

Sir Richard Fairey

John Sheridan

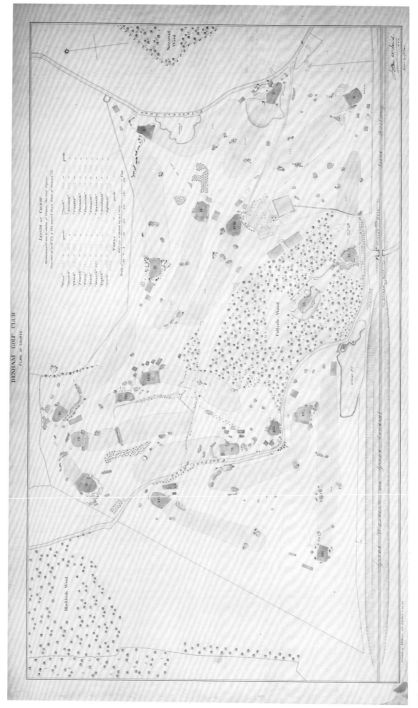

The 1921 course

The 12th green from the tee

The 11th green

A mixed foursome in 1992

The shelter presented by Sir Richard Fairey

The swoop down to the 11th

The 5th green from the 6th tee

The 12th green

Sheridan's house

Two aspects of the clubhouse

9 Post-War Problems

B Y THE second half of 1944 thought was being given by sporting bodies, not least golf clubs, as to what should happen after the war. To some members still engaged overseas in Burma or Italy or in prisoner-of-war camps this may have seemed somewhat premature but as the British and American armies streamed across northern France, there was certainly a possibility that peace might come before the end of 1944.

Denham Golf Club, now master of its lands and with a new constitution, had been taking a cautious look into the future and by the time that the AGM of 1945 arrived, in the last month of the war in Europe, had taken the first steps on the road back to normality. Matches had been played against Oxford and Cambridge Universities, which had long been regarded by Jack Moir as sources of new members. The Tarleton Cup and other competitions had been revived. Mr Moir became a director and also the hon. treasurer. Mr Turberville Smith stepped down after five years as captain – to be succeeded by R.B. Templeton, who had also played a big part in the war-time running of the club and was one of its best golfers.

At the AGM Mr Templeton said that conditions in the club had suffered many changes. Membership, he said, had fallen from 500 to less than 300. Many old members had gone and it had not been possible to retain the old social side of the club 'because every one was interested in the golfing world'. He hoped that it would be possible to restore the old atmosphere in time and that the standard of eligibility of candidates for membership would be jealously maintained.

What the newer members listening to him thought about this is unclear – probably that it referred to someone else.

Mr Templeton foresaw that the next four years would be a period of great difficulty. He hoped that the lady members would help by building up their membership to its pre-war strength. It was his hope, and that of his committee, that the Denham Artisan Golf Club should be encouraged and helped to continue. At this, Major Way chipped in to express the hope that membership of the Artisan Golf Club should be restricted to residents of Denham, a matter close to his heart. The captain agreed, but in 1949, at the request of Mr Sims, hon. secretary of the Artisan Club, the boundary line for membership was extended to a radius of 3 miles from the clubhouse. This required an amendment to rule 3 of the Artisan Club which in 1945 had read: 'Membership shall be open to male Artisans over the age of 18, residing in Denham Parish or, if not so residing, being in the employ of the Denham Golf Club or being a regular caddie engaged by members of the Club, whose election shall be subject to the approval of the Denham Golf Club.'

The Denham Artisan Club was soon given permission to arrange its own fixtures, subject to the availability of the course, and in June 1948 was authorised to increase its membership from 25 to 30. One new member to benefit from this extension was Mr V.E. Balls, whose future must have been as happy as anyone could wish. In the *Buckinghamshire Advertiser* of 1 May 1991 Victor and Nellie Balls were to be seen with a telegram from the Queen congratulating them on their diamond wedding.

Mr Eves, now the derequisition wizard, was frequently on call as Denham Golf Club disentangled itself from the fairly gentle clutches of the Air Ministry. The war was still not quite over when he reported that he had inspected the furniture which had now been returned after storage with Messrs Suters, and found nothing serious enough to justify a claim. On the premises already derequisitioned he had arrived at a figure of £816 in his estimate of the cost of reconditioning.

Derequisitioning was soon not going fast enough for the committee and, encouraged by a statement by Mr Turberville Smith that 'certain matters had come to his knowledge', he and Mr Egerton Johnson were requested to 'make contact at the highest possible level in order to find out the earliest possible date for the derequisition of part of the golf course'.

Meanwhile the indefatigable Mr Eves reported that he had agreed a final settlement (£921 2s 4d) for claims arising out of the requisition of the club house and he was apparently advancing on other fronts as well. This was the heyday of the squatter and he advised the committee that the Ladies' cottage, though short of power points and heating, should be opened for the ladies forthwith to avoid catching the eagle eye of the Local Health Authority.

In July 1947 Mr Eves explained to the committee the position of the claim against the Air Ministry. It was left entirely in his hands to finalise the matter at whatever figure he thought fit. He rarely left a committee meeting without receiving an enthusiastic vote of thanks for his latest coup. He received another when the claim of £2,903 11s 6d in September was finalised and he was made an honorary life member in recognition.

In 1949 he was wrestling with the Town and Country Planning Act and the loss of Development Rights. In April 1950, alas, he died. Some bits and pieces of claims were not yet settled but the club wrote to his firm W. and F. Eves saying 'we shall be very pleased for you to receive any fee which may be payable from the Central Land Board.'

In 1945 Major Way had expressed his willingness 'to ascertain whether it might be possible to purchase the land now or formerly used as a private aerodrome'. But though nothing seems to have come of this, the generosity of Major Way remained staggering. Hereabouts he sent the club a cheque for £150 to mark the 35th anniversary of his association with it.

In November 1946 the committee decided to revive the Mixed Foursomes Competition. The cup was then found to have been lost in the mists of war but Major Way promptly stepped in and offered to present two new cups for the competition which bears his name today.

Another cup which had been mislaid required a more exhaustive search as it was the property of the BB and O. Denham had been the winners in 1939 when it was last contested. Eventually it was decided that it might be in the safe in the linen cupboard. But the key to the safe was also missing. The makers, Messrs Chubb were consulted.

Whether or not it revealed any hidden treasure is not clear but Messrs Chubb were soon being asked about how to dispose of an old safe. Their advice presumably was to advertise it in the *Daily Telegraph*. This was done but brought no definite offers and Mr Walter Henderson offered to see if he could dispose of the safe in the City.

A month later the committee decided to discontinue buying the *Daily Telegraph*!

For more than a year after the war ended the club was chary of encouraging societies to play at Denham. Catering restrictions were going to exist for a long time and the profusion of committee meetings, and their length, testified to how much ground there was to make up.

At the AGMs of 1946 and 1947 Colonel Wyld was still in the chair but he died in the following spring. He had been the last survivor of the seven founders. In the 38 years since the meeting at Savay Farm, (which Oswald Mosley had renamed Savehay Farm) Colonel Wyld had taken a prominent part in the life of the club, even while still managing director of Fortnum and Mason. During the war he was said to have ridden to meetings from the Tile House on his horse.

Walter Henderson followed Colonel Wyld as the chairman. Jack Moir was the hon. treasurer. Mr Templeton had been followed as captain by C.K.F. (later Sir Kenneth) Hague, after whom came Major H.C.M. Stone and then Jack Moir. Mr Moir was to become the leading figure in the running of Denham Golf Club until his death in 1983.

The steward and stewardess, Mr and Mrs Brayley, who had clearly worked miracles in keeping the club going through the war, had to resign through Mrs Brayley's ill health. Their son and his wife took over but only briefly.

The Denham side against Cambridge University in 1947. It contains many names which feature in this history. (left to right, standing): *D.C. Grant, R.H. Hollis, A.R. Robson, F.S. Harrison (Hon. Secretary), D.F. Burns, H.R. Minchin, B.J.B. Sloley;* (seated) *C.F.K. Hague, Sir Giles Scott, H.H.R. Browne, Major H.C.M. Stone, J.H. Butler, J.W.J. Moir*

In October 1946 the secretary, Mr Shield, resigned and was made an hon. member of the club. The minutes of the committee meeting on that Sunday morning record that a member F.S. Harrison, who had spent much of his working life in the Far East, was in attendance. He was then asked to take over as hon. secretary. To this he agreed with the stipulation that it should be for not longer than six months until a full-time secretary should be appointed.

'Harry' Harrison remained the hon. secretary for 17 years. He was a rare character, brusque but kindly, and was much missed when he died, still in office, in 1963. He is remembered with particular affection by young members of the time. After a few initial grumbles, he would almost always support them and their complaints and suggestions.

Mr Hague's year of captaincy was an eventful one, for it covered the appointments of a new secretary, a new steward and a new professional. Mr Hague's son Nigel, on his installation as captain at the AGM 27 years later (with Sir Kenneth present a few months before his death), reminded the meeting of the historical dangers of appointing a Hague as captain, but fortunately his year proved tranquil and comparatively uneventful.

Early in 1946 A.J. Miles, the professional, had retired and the general committee had appointed the greens committee to select a successor. Nigel Hague recounts how one of the great selections was made:

> The PGA was informed of the vacancy and over 80 applications were received, including some from the well known professionals of the day. The greens committee (Messrs Hague, Moir, W.R. Trounson and Major Stone) decided that they wanted someone who had been in the Services during the war and whittled down the number of candidates to 32. It was arranged that all 32 should be interviewed on eight separate days at my father's office in Faringdon Street. He was then managing director of Babcock and Wilcox Ltd. The first four were due to be interviewed on Derby Day.
>
> Meanwhile John Sheridan, son of the celebrated caddie-master at Sunningdale, Jimmy Sheridan, had recently been demobbed. Before the war he had been an assistant at Swinley Forest and Sunningdale but now wanted a full professional's job. He was told by Commander Roe, then secretary of the PGA, that Denham were looking for somebody but were unlikely to be interested in him.
>
> Nevertheless John decided to apply, just for the experience. But he had also decided to fulfil an ambition by attending the Derby that year and indeed on the previous Sunday had walked the course in the company of the professional at the RAC, Epsom. However, when John arrived home, his father told him that he had to go to an interview at 5.30 pm on the afternoon of the race. John at first demurred and a family altercation ensued. But Jimmy Sheridan's word was law and John had to miss the Derby.
>
> John was the third of the four applicants to be interviewed on that day. Immediately the fourth had left, one member of the greens committee said: 'Well, we want that chap Sheridan, don't we?' The other three all immediately agreed and there was no further discussion. The decision was made in a matter of seconds. John was told next day that he had got the job.

In the search for new members the committee wrote to the hon. secretary of Oxhey Golf Club, which was closing down, and invited him to introduce any one who might be eligible as a candidate for membership of Denham. Towards the end of 1947 a new clamp-down on petrol brought a new increase in resignations but Mr Moir was able to lessen the impact by pointing out the closeness of the course to Denham Golf Club Halt, which had just survived an attempt to rename it Higher Denham. Sir Michael Barrington-Ward, a local resident and member of the Railway Executive, was popularly given the credit for the successful defence of the title.

A Jeep tractor was put out of use by the petrol shortage but Mr Mullins, a local farmer, did a lot of work on the course in 1947 and 1948, especially in cutting the long grass. In return the club let him graze his cattle to the left of the 14th fairway subject to the provision of a substantial fence, at an annual rental of £1.

Another shortage at this time seems to have been of whisky but a decision to reintroduce a ration of two doubles a week was soon reversed on the urgings of the house committee.

It may surprise the younger members of today that as late as 1948 the country of the Old Berkeley Hunt stretched as far as Denham, indeed the MFH sent £5 to compensate the club for damage done. Hounds were, in fact, still meeting at Horn Hill ten years later and could be heard only just over the hill from the 14th tee, to the consternation no doubt of the old dog fox who used to live in the bunker on the right of the 14th.

Life for the reader of the Denham Golf Club archives becomes sweeter with the advent of Harry Harrison in 1947, for he was equipped with a typewriter. The struggle of reading eccentric and varied handwriting is over. So is the brief absence from the records of the name of Sir Giles Gilbert Scott.

It was early in 1947 that the firm of A. and J. Sims reported decay in the woodwork of the club house. The committee's instant reaction was to ask Sir Giles to submit a report on the extent of the damage, done allegedly by beetles, and the best method of dealing with it and with them.

A fortnight later they had not only Sir Giles's report but Sir Giles in person. It was if he had been merely marking time rebuilding the House of Commons while waiting to be invited to sort out the Denham beetles. He agreed to send an expert, after whose inspection the hon. secretary would employ a firm to carry out the work needed. At the next meeting it was decided to appoint Messrs A. and J. Sims, if Sir Giles approved of the firm. Sir Giles did, which was bad news for the beetles.

The increasing vulnerability of golf clubs to theft and their need for alertness at all times was demonstrated fairly early in John Sheridan's career at Denham. Having watched a powerfully built stranger hovering around the locker room, he challenged him. The man ran off into the wood beside the 18th fairway pursued by Messrs Sheridan, Butcher (the steward) and Hester, an artisan.

Mr Butcher, late of the Royal Marines, seems to have directed a skilful outflanking movement and they eventually pinned down the offender on the 6th fairway. He missed with a punch at Sheridan which, according to the target, would have ended a promising career there and then if it had connected, but the former marine was in his element and they brought the quarry back to the clubhouse and handed him over to the police. The going rate in 1948 for such a successful defence of Denham's and Denham members' property seems to have been £3 per head.

Later Sheridan had a brilliantly vigilant disciple (well-trained, he says) in his assistant Michael Brothers who was for ever alert and had a hot line to the local CID. On one occasion he worked out that breakages into cars were occurring at lunch time on Wednesdays and Thursdays and coincided with the appearance of a character whom he would know again. He watched and, when the suspect next turned up, Brothers phoned the police who told him to try to block the man's exit. This he did by driving his car across the exit from the overflow car park. In trying to escape, the suspect crashed his car and was duly arrested. He was found to be carrying 115 car keys and his house in Northwood had a store of golf equipment which Messrs Lillywhite's might have envied. (In 1979 Michael Brothers became the professional at Beaconsfield where he is no doubt equally popular with members and no less successful in repelling invaders.)

In the 1960s and 1970s John Sheridan and Michael Brothers took over the supply of caddies who by then were mostly boys, more accurately described as bag-carriers or trolley-pullers. The old characters were fading out, though Butterfield, affectionately known as 'Buttercup', was to be seen doing odd jobs around the clubhouse until 1991. He had briefly been caddie-master after the Second World War when he had the task of managing two notable figures in Sharman and Robinson. Nigel Hague recalls:

Sharman survived several brushes with authority. After the war he caddied regularly for members. In fact, he was the best caddy of his time, shrewd and knowledgeable about golf, and he frequently caddied for John Sheridan when John played in professional tournaments.

Robinson was another caddy of great character, quite different from Sharman. 'Robbie' was perhaps more of a bag-carrier than a true caddy but he always took a great interest in any match and threw himself enthusiastically behind the cause of the golfer for whom he was caddying. On one well-remembered occasion, when caddying for Jack Moir, Robbie forgot himself in his excitement and cried out: 'Take your jigger, Jack!' – followed by a contrite 'Oh, beg pardon, sir.' No one could ever get angry with Robbie and Jack Moir was as amused as anyone. For a time 'Take your jigger, Jack' became the vogue phrase among many of the younger members.

Robbie used to sleep rough until Harry Harrison ('the Major' as Robbie always called him) let him sleep in the boiler-house in exchange for doing odd jobs. Robbie was often to be seen around the clubhouse and in the inner sanctum of John Sheridan's shop, a dishevelled but cheerful and lovable character.

10 Freehold

MAJOR Roger Way was on the committee and a director until 1952 and never lost touch with the running of the club. Sometimes the committee called on him for help, as when one member suggested that a felled oak on the right of the 12th should be disposed of and Major Way said he would see the contractors about it next day. Sometimes he wrote to the committee with a suggestion. He was president of the Denham Artisan Golf Club (and of the Denham Bowling Club) and he acted as a link with individual artisan members who had a problem for the golf club committee.

When there was discussion about whether the artisans should be asked to work on the course, it was Major Way who put the matter to the artisans, apparently with gratifying results.

A valuable source of income in the early post-war years was provided by the United States Army Air Force, indeed the hon. treasurer, Jack Moir, went on record as saying that in one or two years their contribution made all the difference between profit and loss. Through Myles Formby, the eminent surgeon who was captain in 1951 and a director of the company, medical students from University College Hospital were also made welcome. So, too, were others from St Mary's.

There was, however, a set-back to the policy of playing matches against Oxford and Cambridge in the hope that they would become a source of new members. One of the pre-war members still to be seen at Denham, though living in the Isle of Wight, is Bill Sloley who recalls the embarrassing morning in 1946 when the University side turned up in their coach – to find that the then Denham secretary had forgotten to raise a Denham side. Members of widely varying ability found themselves being drafted into a Denham team as they arrived for their normal Saturday morning contests until the requisite number was reached. This incident and the poor showing of previous Denham sides against the strong and experienced University sides of the post-war era sank the fixtures almost beyond recall. In Bill Sloley's words: 'It took the Steel brothers, Billy in the Oxford side, Donald at Cambridge, to revive them in the late 50s.'

Bill Sloley also recalled that before the war new members were not allowed to ask any one for a game without the secretary's permission, and lady members applying to join the club had to wear a hat when brought up to meet committee members. He mentions a bomb crater to the left of the 14th fairway and the friendly leg-pulling in 1946 of Christopher Mayhew, a Labour MP who was then Under-Secretary for Foreign Affairs, and later Minister of Defence.

Lord Mayhew, now a Liberal peer, had also been a member of Denham before the war – with his father, Sir Basil – when he was up at Oxford. He is remembered kindly by another Denham member of today for his willingness to turn out and perform the long jump for the Christ Church athletic team.

To help members over the weekends during petrol rationing the room until 1990 used as the secretary's office was available as a bedroom. Many, however, came by train for years after the war and the 5.39 Sunday train to London used to wait for members running across the 11th fairway and ducking under the wire to get on board, the Up platform being still sited 80 yards or so east of its present position.

In the early post-war years Bill Sloley and John Henderson had a lot of trouble in persuading other members of the committee to start a New Year's Eve dance. They asked Sir Giles about siting the band complete with piano over the entrance to the dining-room. He spent some time in measuring but finally rejected it.

One New Year the Cambridge Footlights Dance Band came – organised by a member of Denham who was in the band. Not all the professional bands were a success. Harry Harrison is said to have been most reluctant to pay one of them because so many members complained of the shortage of waltzes.

Bill Sloley supplies one answer to the question often asked by visitors: Have planes taking off from the airfield or landing ever been hit by a golf ball? The answer is – at least three times. Before the runway was constructed there were various lines of approach and departure and J.B. Hague, brother of Sir Kenneth, was known to have hit one with his drive on the 3rd. The ball was lost at first but was later found embedded in the fuselage. Donald Steel hit one with a 9-iron at the 4th but the ball was never seen again. By contrast Mary Braithwaite's drive from the 4th tee rebounded off a plane into the bunker on the left.

The 1950s were the last years of Major Roger Way. Many years later, when new members were coming in at a rate of 50 a year, Jack Moir thought that they should know about the extreme generosity of the Way family and at an AGM cited examples of it. Before the Second War the club had paid a rent of only £600 a year and that was allowed to lapse when war broke out. There was also Major Way's generosity when the course was bought.

This purchase did not include much of the woodland and all the cottages. In time most of these were acquired too and in 1974 Jack Moir could say that the whole of the property had cost £20,000. 'It is today insured for about £230,000,' he said.

On two occasions in the 1950s Major Way offered a section of woodland on very favourable terms and Mr Moir as chairman said that the golf club must buy it to protect its amenities. The first was near the Halt, the other on the right of the 17th.

For some years the committee had been brooding on Development Rights and had asked a member, Mr C.W. Stothert, to clarify the position. He told them that until the club applied to the authorities for permission to build, the question of receiving any compensation for loss of Development Rights did not arise. If the application was turned down, then the club would be in a position to lodge a claim. But not otherwise.

This same year, the USAF arranged for five members of the US Walker Cup team to fly down and play Denham after their match. Dick Scott (extreme left) *and John Sheridan* (extreme right) *won their match against Dale Morey and Billy Joe Patton* (in glasses). *Patton had failed to tie for the Masters by a single stroke the previous year. The Denham men are shown receiving their winnings, autographed £1 notes. Alas, Dick Scott, in an absent-minded moment, paid for a round of drinks with his note and it was never traced*

In October 1955 an EGM was held. Wages, the cost of repairs and the outlay for future building programmes had forced a special finance sub-committee to recommend a rise in the men's subscription to 18 guineas for those over 35, for ladies to 14 guineas. The entrance fee for full members and five-day members was to be reintroduced at half the annual subscription.

In the chair was J.H. (Pa) Butler, father of Reub, who greatly resembled him. Pa was that year's captain. He had stood in as hon. secretary for six months in 1949–50 when Harry Harrison, went to New Zealand. The chairman explained that the reason for calling the meeting was to acquaint members with the finances of the club and to give them a chance to discuss them in the light of the subscription increases. The rest he left to Jack Moir.

Mr Moir pointed out the increases in expenditure to be expected in the future. The ground staff was a man short. One would have to be found accommodation. A pension fund for the staff had soon to be considered and his estimates did not include the pay of a secretary in the event of the hon. secretary retiring in the near future. (The last four words were heavily deleted from the minutes, suggesting that this was the last thing that the hon. secretary intended.)

Mr Moir added that the charge for societies would be increased from 15s to £1 a head, which is always music to members' ears. Among the subjects discussed subsequently was that of ladies using the main bar at week-ends after a certain hour, though whether this was expected to revive the falling bar profits was not clear.

In 1956 Major Way wrote asking if the club would be prepared to buy another 4.7 acres of land on the right of the 17th fairway. Though government land was valued at £50 an acre, he would let the club have it for £200.

In Mr Moir's words the club 'had no option' and the purchase was completed. Major Way then wrote a letter which really set the wheels of power moving. He asked why the club had never put in a claim for loss of Development Rights. At a time of financial worries this struck a note of some urgency and the committee asked Colonel Frank Trumper, a chartered surveyor not long retired as senior partner of Cluttons, 'to look into the matter'. The colonel, who was also engaged at the time in designing a club tie, was authorised to prepare various applications for development, one of them seeking permission to build two cottages below the garages.

Colonel Trumper had a mild set-back in the design for the club tie (which the committee at first rejected on the grounds that the dove was too large) but he submitted two planning applications to the Eton Rural District Council and one of them, that for the cottages behind the garages, seemed on course to be granted.

The colonel was warmly thanked by that year's captain, Roger Hollis, of whom it need only be said that the doubts cast on his patriotism 25 years later were utterly discounted by Denham members who knew him best, indeed were regarded as laughable. During his years on the Denham committee, Sir Roger Hollis met many prospective members who, on learning that the affable member to whom they had been talking in the bar was the head of MI5, must have thought that this really was a most exclusive golf club.

What with Colonel Trumper hunting Development Rights and Mr Stothert

Sir Roger Hollis (left) *and J.W.J. Moir*

in pursuit of a fair rating assessment, the committee were in sight of two promising sources of financial relief. In July 1957 the colonel reported that the authorities had agreed to settle the club's claim for £8,114 3s 4d. He thought that this was not enough and pressed on until he secured a final assessment of £9,371 8s 7d.

On this winning note Jack Moir resigned as hon. treasurer to be succeeded by Derrick Walker, who had been groomed for the part for some time. But the claim for a rates reassessment was lost and the settlement for Development Rights had no immediate effect on the club's finances. Mr Moir warned that Mr Turberville Smith, who had drawn up the debenture deed, was of the opinion that the money belonged to the debenture holders. The club sought independent views and counsel's opinion and the arguments rumbled on for some years.

Eventually a solution was found through the persuasiveness of Harry Harrison. He could do nothing about those debentures now held by trustees after the death of the holders, but he could approach existing members with an offer of a reduction in annual subscriptions in return for their surrendering their debentures. This was successful and the balance was sufficient to build the two cottages behind the garages.

In November 1957 Major Roger Way died, aged 79. Few non-golfers can ever have contributed so much to the pleasure of golfers as he did. His widow Brenda was made an honorary life member.

The future of Oakleigh Cottage, the house on the left as one climbs up from the 12th green, was still unsettled. The club was keen to buy it but Major Way had retained it until the future plans of his son Lewis with his young family were determined. By 1960, Oakleigh had been bought and the decision about who should live in it had to be made. Jack Moir summed up the situation at a meeting of the general committee in August.

'In my opinion', he said, 'the order of preference in any club is, firstly, the secretary, secondly the steward and thirdly the professional. I feel, however, that in view of John Sheridan's long connection with the club and having in view the excellent work he has done in the last 14 years, he deserves some special consideration above the normal.'

So that was settled.

11 Denham and the Arts

AMONG the minor differences between Denham Golf Club and the local authorities had been one about the siting of a direction sign at the junction of Tilehouse Lane and the North Orbital Road. The Eton Rural District Council said that it was not their responsibility.

Early in the Second World War all sign posts throughout the country had been removed in order to baffle any enemy agents who might be dropping in by parachute, some, it was rumoured, dressed as nuns. Many direction signs were not immediately restored in 1945 after the war and even the natives sometimes had difficulty in knowing where they were. So it was that on the first occasion that John McCallum came to play at Denham, in 1948, he could not find it and was very late for a game with Roger Livesey and his wife Ursula Jeans.

The Liveseys, then in their heyday on stage and screen, were a most popular couple in the club. They were not the greatest golfers and McCallum was impressed on this occasion by the ease with which his host lost three balls in the rough on the right when they started at the 10th. Once, apparently, Livesey had lost six balls from the 1st tee at Sunningdale.

Mervyn Johns and the film director, Anthony Asquith were keen members at one time but since the early days of Denham Golf Club the theatre had not been strongly represented in the membership. Rex Harrison, when married to Lilli Palmer, lived in The Little House behind the 6th tee and became a member in 1944 but there is no evidence that he played much golf. John Mills, who followed him in the house, did play but moved away after a time. Sir John returned to live in Denham Village and in the 1990s, when he was over 80, was still to be seen striding up the fairway accompanied by a small dog.

In the early 1950s John McCallum and his wife, Googie Withers, moved into The Mirrie, which is the lovely-looking house halfway up the 5th. For the benefit of members who have only seen it from the course, this is how John saw it, looking out, in his book *Life with Googie*:

> It was a William and Mary style house, built about 1910. It faced south on to a rose garden and then on to a beautiful stretch of the golf course. It was set in three and a

half acres, mostly apple orchard, with a grass tennis court and a large kitchen garden. A lovely cedar of Lebanon shaded the southern end of the tennis court and a path ran under it to a stile on to the golf course. It was a beautiful house and garden, in a lovely English setting, and we were very happy there.

Joanna McCallum, then about four, had been used to a life of touring, and gave the seal of approval to their new residence. On surveying The Mirrie for the first time she proclaimed it the best hotel they had been in and asked her father if they could stay on.

One of the best remembered incidents of the 1950s occurred when Harry Harrison found the spirited Italian wife of a member sitting in a bunker by the 5th green while her two children played in the sand with their buckets and spades. McCallum recalls her dashing husband Hugh Nisbett 'hitting a ball into the then Ladies' loo from the 10th tee and, his bravery fortified by Warrior Port, retrieving it.'

While the McCallum family lived in The Mirrie, their next door neighbours at The Little House were Mr and Mrs Trepte, who came home one Sunday afternoon to find a pantechnicon in the drive and four men calmly loading it with all their furniture and belongings. Fortunately the Treptes were able to block the drive and call the police.

One of the characters in the neighbourhood at that time was Jock, the porter–ticket collector–stationmaster of Denham Golf Club Halt whom Bill Sloley remembers as bringing *The Times* up to the clubhouse every morning. He was on duty in the early morning when the commuters, including Sir Michael Barrington-Ward, a member of the Railway Executive, went off to London and he was there when John McCallum, then playing in the West End, arrived back on the last train well after midnight.

> One night Joe was behaving very strangely. He had his cap on for one thing, and his buttons were polished and done up for another. I generally stopped for a minute or two to have a chat with him – he was a cheerful little fellow – but this night he seemed very preoccupied and said to me rather brusquely, 'Excuse me sir, I'm busy', which was an astonishing enough statement in itself. I stood aside and watched him, fascinated. He picked up a hurricane lamp and peered up the line. An express was approaching. Jock stood stiffly to attention, hurricane lamp held high, shoulders back. The express thundered through. All the carriages were sleepers, curtains drawn, because at that hour most of the passengers would be asleep. When it had passed, Jock lowered his lantern and relaxed. 'Sorry, sir', he said to me. 'But you see,' he added, looking after the disappearing train, 'that was the Queen.'

John McCallum was prised away from the Shangri-la of The Mirrie on being appointed managing-director in Melbourne of J.C. Williamson Ltd, the biggest theatrical organisation in the world. He sold the property to Mr P.B. Johnsen, who still lives there and has been a member of the club since 1959. His wife and two sons are also members. When in London, McCallum, one of the world's most enthusiastic and best preserved golfers, seldom misses a chance of playing at Denham, albeit not without a wistful look over the hedge at the 5th.

In 1962 the club's finances were helped by the filming on the course of a sequence from a Bob Hope film *Call Me Bwana*. While the cameras were busy around the 6th green, Arnold Palmer is said to have strolled across to the 17th tee and to have hit a ball from there on to the 17th green. Opinions vary as to which tee he was on and what club he used. The authority on the subject must be John Sheridan and he says that it was the ladies tee and a wooden club. The sequence being filmed was cut out of the version seen in the United Kingdom.

12 The Ladies

BEFORE 1914 there were far more lady golfers in Britain than is popularly supposed. The pictures which survive, showing them clad in a way which would impair the most fluent swing, suggest that they were isolated pioneers. But Bob Fenning's delving into the files of the ladies' section shows that its members were well organised and played a valuable part in the establishing of Denham Golf Club. He writes:

The first General Meeting of the Denham Ladies Golf Club took place on 20 April 1912 when it was resolved to have a committee of eight together with the captain who was to be *ex officio*. Mrs Peel-Smith took the chair and one of the ladies present was Mrs F. Woodbridge, making even more definite the connection of the Woodbridge family with Denham Golf Club. It was at that meeting that it was decided to ask the directors to provide a monthly medal at a cost which should not exceed 5 shillings. In June of that year, the committee wrote to the club asking whether the directors would amend Rule 20 to read '50 Lady Playing Members'. It is a pity that there is no copy of the first rule book.

That ladies played a part in the development of the club in its early days there is no doubt. In fact, the first two names in the candidates book were a Mrs J.C. Macro Wilson and a Mrs Phipps who were elected provisional members. The first honorary life member was Mrs Isabel Way, mother of Colonel Ben Way and his brothers, Gerald and Roger. She died in 1913.

The ladies held their first medal on 6 June 1912. It was won by Mrs Janson with 107–32 = 75. The first inter-club match was held at Denham on 17 October 1912 against West Drayton. Denham won it 6–2. The men had held their first match on 15 May 1912 against Barclays Bank.

It is interesting that on 3 October 1912 the committee decided that in the event of a match being all square after 18 holes in a club competition, the first three holes should

Constricting golf wear of the time — what Burberrys were advertising in 1912

be played and, if still all square, continue to the best of three holes. These were the same conditions as those that until recently existed in the Tarleton Cup.

Much discussion took place just after the First World War over the question of a ladies' club room. The original plan for the clubhouse showed the ladies' changing room being next to the men's with the ladies' lounge being the end part of what is now the mixed lounge. But at some time previously it had become the men's smoking room and it was 1920 before the ladies were allowed to use it from Monday to Friday. There is little doubt that the changing rooms for both ladies and men were totally inadequate but it was not until 1935 that the ladies agreed by 23 votes to 4 to move to the old steward's cottage. It was agreed that a covered way should be built between the clubhouse and the cottage. The ladies stayed there until 1990 but no covered way was ever built.

In the 1930s Denham Ladies Golf Club was very active. Monthly medal and bogey competitions were held and matches were played against local clubs on a regular basis. The best player between the wars was Cecil Leitch, though she was near the end of her wonderful career when she came to live with her sister in Denham and joined the golf club. Starting in 1908 when, aged 17, she reached the semi-final of the British Ladies Championship at St Andrews, she won the French Ladies Championship five times, the British four times, the English twice and the Canadian Open once – in 1921 when in the final she beat the unfortunate Mrs M. M'Bride 17 and 15. After the First World War her matches with Joyce Wethered were among the most exciting sporting events of the day.

Cecil Leitch during her peak years, in around 1920. She was one of the first women golfers to hit really hard. By this time, you can see golf wear was far more suitable

In later years she presented the club with a model and the Cecil Leitch Trophy is played for annually.

During the Second World War there were great difficulties in keeping the club going and it was largely due to the efforts of Mrs J.L. Whitaker, who became a member in 1926, that the club survived and recovered so well after the war. She died only in 1992.

In 1991 Mrs Whitaker, who was made an honorary life member in 1929 and was still resident in Marsham Way, Gerrards Cross, was invited to contribute from her memories of Denham. She responded most kindly and wrote as follows:

In the 1920s, I used to drive my husband to Denham with Harry Harrison, when he was home on leave, and Frankie Chancellor. We would collect old Mr Coles from Denham Mount and the caddies were lined up waiting for them.

As one looked back from the clubhouse there was not a trace of anything before Denham Station apart from the two big houses at the entrance (now Cilla Black's).

The ladies' quarters were very cramped and to reach them we had to walk past the men's and were then where the extension to the lounge now is. We then got promoted to the old cottage which had been the boiler house.

The secretary was Colonel Hales; the bar was the holy of holies; the catering was wonderfully done by Mr and Mrs Debnam with Mrs Lipscombe to help at weekends. Denham was renowned for its excellent food, especially Mrs Debnam's fruit cake.

Most of the lovely old houses in Denham belonged to members. At the beginning of the Second World War, Denham Place was occupied by Lord Vansittart who moved a lot of his staff from London, I think for security reasons, and housed them in the top floors.

One of the outstanding characters of Denham, Miss Kersey, was known as the Denham Greyhound. Always immaculately dressed in shirt and tie, trousers and with an Eton crop, she was the most impatient person. I remember her getting more and more enraged on the 5th tee waiting for an extremely slow men's foursome to move off the green. Eventually she charged ahead and, when she caught up with them, was let through for the sake of peace. At first I was terrified of her but was very fond of her in her old age. Leslie and I used to visit her regularly with a bottle of her favourite tipple!

In the Old Rectory the two Misses Selby ran a domestic science school. When Martin Bakers and other big firms settled in Higher Denham, the narrow Rectory Lane became too dangerous and that was when the old Up platform was closed.

At the end of the War Sir Kenneth Hague made me take over and try to get things going, not easy as few records had been kept. I started by trying to get the lounge cleaned. It was filthy, not having been used. I then hoped to cheer it up with curtains and so on but was firmly refused, as this would make the room too 'pansy'! How different today when it is all so cheerful and attractive! Next we had to try to get some players and as usual John Sheridan was brilliant in giving lessons. Some had never held a club. We held an Open Invitation Day, which was a great success. Helped by the Secretary and by John Sheridan and Pa and Reub Butler, my husband Leslie and I were then able to get some sort of team and arrange matches.

When Sir Miles Bickerton offered the airfield land for, I think, £3,000, my husband, who was not on the committee but, being both barrister and chartered accountant, always gave excellent advice, felt that Denham had no practice ground, and the club should buy the extra land to make room for one. Had they followed his advice, there would have been no aerodrome or its club for Denham – and the neighbourhood would have been much more peaceful.

One of the greatest improvements was extending the bar and giving everyone somewhere to have a snack lunch. I hope very much that the original cartoons will remain prominent. They were excellent caricatures – and I could recognise them all.

The snag about buying what is now the airfield was that Denham Golf Club at that time was still only a tenant of the Way family.

The relationship between men's and ladies' sections seems to have nearly always been marvellously harmonious and has stayed so, with none of the scrapping which, if the Sunday papers are to be believed, goes on in other parts of the country.

Though the official figure of lady full members was said to be 75, there were times in the 1950s when there were fewer than a dozen regular playing members. Even in the late 1960s and early 1970s there was sometimes only one girl junior member.

The first impact of the Denham ladies outside Bucks was made by Marigold Speir, a pupil of John Sheridan's from when she started playing at the age of 15. Having played for Bucks between 1951 and 1953 and won the County Championship of 1953, she returned to Scotland with her parents and in 1957 won the Scottish Ladies Championship at Troon, beating Mrs Helen Holm of Troon in the final. In the 1990s she was still living in St Andrews and in touch with Ray Sherning, who herself belies the fact that in 1992 she will have been a member for 40 years.

Whereas on the men's side there had been doubts about the usefulness of the BB and O, the ladies had been on the best of terms with the Bucks Ladies between the wars, no doubt partly through the services to the county of a Denham member, Mrs Nancy Gold.

Mrs Gold played for Bucks between 1925 and 1958, was county champion ten times between 1928 and 1951, captain in 1927–8 and 1932 and president in 1965. By the 1950s she had been joined in county representative matches by several other Denham members.

Mrs Patience Whitworth-Jones played from 1947 to 1951 and reappeared later as Mrs D.H.R. Martin to play between 1955 and 1969. Mrs Betty Stothert, whose husband was the recipient of many a vote of thanks from the Denham committee for his battle over the rates, played for Bucks between 1953 and 1956, was champion in 1955 and captain in 1953–4. Mrs Hilda Hartley Clark played in the early 1950s when Mrs Enid Daniel was the Bucks captain.

It was the arrival of Mrs Mary Braithwaite in 1957 which started Denham on a rising tide until they became the strongest club in Bucks ladies' golf. She played for the county between 1956 and 1983, was captain in 1962 and 1967 and president in 1980–2. She won the County Championship in 1961 and was still good enough to be runner-up in 1975. In the final at Stoke Poges that year she played the 17-year-old Lynn Harrold of Gerrards Cross, whose subsequent playing career as a professional was to be ended so cruelly by a motor-cycle accident in America which cost her the loss of an eye.

By the 1970s Denham ladies, mostly young mothers, were so prominent in the county's golf that they supplied three of the four semi-finalists in the Bucks Championship. Barbara Dutton, née Trumper, was county champion in 1965, Jenny Marshall in 1972 and Gilly Gordon in 1973 when the final was played in teeming rain at Denham. The Bucks lady captains after Mary Braithwaite included Meg Moeran 1968–9, Tina Dresher 1973–4, Jenny Marshall 1977–8, Jill Yarrow 1979–80, Barbara Fox (formerly Dutton) 1987–8 and Carol Ritchie 1991–2.

Outside the county, the most notable successes were the three victories in the London Foursomes recorded by Mary Braithwaite, the first two with Barbara Dutton in 1965 and 1967. They won first at Denham and, after missing 1966 while Barbara was on maternity leave, triumphed again at West Herts where in miserable weather they beat Sunningdale Ladies (Glenna Campbell and a formidable Australian Pamela Greaves) in the final by 6 and 5. 'Throughout the event', wrote Enid Wilson in the *Daily Telegraph*, 'they adhered rigidly to the golden rule of foursomes play, namely keeping the ball on the fairway, and they putted well.'

Mary Braithwaite's partner when Denham won again, at Ashford Manor in 1973, was Angela Uzielli, whose greatest achievements still lay some way ahead. At about this time Angela and John Uzielli, having moved to Ascot, joined The Berkshire. However, when she won the British Championship she was made an honorary life member of Denham and, far from going into decline with the passing years, went on to win the English Championship at the age of 50.

The successes of this generation were followed up in the next. Parental support and example may be the basic stimuli but by the 1980s Denham juniors were also being given every opportunity to play golf – and enjoy it – in the school holidays with group classes and competitions organised by Ian and Maureen McCaskill and Sir Scott and Lady Baker in conjunction with John Sheridan.

In the 1980s Fiona Walkinshaw and Nicola Marshall played for Bucks, took Denham to the final of the London Foursomes, and made history while at Cambridge by playing for the Stymies. They narrowly missed being the first girls to win a Blue. Fiona captained the Stymies.

Their respective parents, Jim and Margaret Walkinshaw and Robin and Jenny Marshall, had, of course, to take a bow for handing down the academic prowess nowadays required to get into Oxford or Cambridge. The subsequent achievements in this field of Donald and Rosie Chilvers, parents of Angus Chilvers, the Oxford captain of 1988, and then of Hamish and Carol Ritchie, Norman and Sarah Hampel and John and Jenny Sanders, who between them accounted for three members of the Oxford side of 1991 in Stuart Ritchie, Johnny Hampel and Richard Sanders, speaks volumes for the IQ of modern Denham members.

In the years after the Second World War the ladies section settled at 75 full members from which it eventually rose to 100. In the 1980s there was something of an explosion and a brake had to be put on to keep the numbers at 125. Occasionally the general committee had discussed the idea of inviting the lady captain or her representative to join the committee *ex officio* but, like the General Synod of the Church of England, they could not quite bring themselves to take the plunge. Eventually in May 1979 they did, with no known ill effects to any one.

This seems to be a suitable place to record the services to Denham Golf Club, which is very much a family club, of one particular family, the Trumpers. Mrs Trumper is said to have been a doughty lady who rode a bicycle to Denham from Wimbledon before the First War. Her son, Colonel Frank Trumper, was captain in 1963, his wife Freda was lady captain in 1955 and 1966. In the next generation their son John and their daughter Barbara more than maintained the family record. John was captain in 1985, his wife Sorrel lady captain in 1990.

Barbara, for many years one of the best players in the county, was lady captain of Denham in 1977, the same year that her husband Peter Dutton was captain. Peter Dutton's death aged 35, halfway through his year of office, was felt deeply throughout the club. A fine golfer, unusually long for an amateur and a popular figure, he was much missed and his family's grief was shared by all.

However, another generation of Trumpers and Duttons has already moved on from junior membership – and there is clearly a lot of mileage left in their elders.

13 Sources

BEFORE 1960 the membership of Denham Golf Club had not included many Scots. One, Sir William Christie, was prominent on the committee but he arrived not from north of the Border but from east of Suez. He had been a senior civil servant in India. Jack Moir, of course, was another Scot but he had lived in the neighbourhood since boyhood. As hon. treasurer for many years after the Second World War and three times captain, he had a guiding hand behind most of the club's activities. Billy and Donald Steel had been at school at Fettes but lived at Hillingdon. Their father, Dr W. Arkley Steel, a much respected member, was the inspiration behind the new Hillingdon Hospital.

The gathering of the clans seems to have quickened from the election in 1961 of Robin Marshall, whose father was an old friend of Jack Moir's. After living for a time in Denham Green, Robin and Jenny Marshall moved to The Thatched Cottage which is seen through the trees from the 12th. As a rugby footballer, a lively wing forward who played in a Scottish final trial, Robin was in the London Scottish seven which won the Middlesex Sevens at Twickenham four years running in the early 1960s. So was Jim Shackleton who joined Denham later. Shackleton went on to play in the next two finals, both against Loughborough Colleges, the first lost, the second, in 1965, won when a Scottish seven also included two other future Denham members, Tim Percival and Stewart Wilson.

Thereafter many young Scottish golfers and their charming wives arrived at Denham, most of them with a native talent for the game and a more thorough grounding in it then is given elsewhere.

By the 1970s the link with rugby football had led to the presence of eleven internationals in the membership of Denham – three English (Ted Woodward, Bill Patterson and the late John Currie); two Irish (Jim Murphy-O'Connor and Jimmy Ritchie); five Scottish (Frans ten Bos, Jim Shackleton, Gordon MacDonald, Hamish Inglis and Stewart Wilson); and one Welsh (Malcolm Thomas).

It became a normal progression for young Scots coming south to work in London to join Denham. They undoubtedly raised the standard of golf in the club, male and female.

One of the best amateurs in Scotland had already come south to Denham in 1957. Michael Dawson graced the club until in the 1970s his job required a move to the other side of London. He joined Rye and in due course became captain there. He remains an honorary life member of Denham. Two other fine golfers to follow were Robert Walker, a most distinguished member of Prestwick and a leading light of the Old Salopians during their best years in the Halford Hewitt, and Jim Walkinshaw, in the 1990s the chairman of Denham Golf Club Limited.

It was Robert Walker who in his year of office as captain, 1989, decided that this history should be written. He also decided who should write it, which some may see as the only blot on his otherwise unblemished career. Jim Walkinshaw had his handicap reduced to scratch when he was several years into his 50s, setting an example to one and all.

Other high class golfers to be found at Denham in the 1950s and 1960s were: Peter and David Dutton; Dick Scott, son of Sir Giles and not only the architect of many Charterhouse successes on the golf course but of the school's new buildings; Richard Braddon, another Carthusian, who had won the Boys Championship at Moortown and remained a very good player despite a protesting back; and Air Vice-Marshal Cecil Beamish. Anyone who found the air vice-marshal a difficult opponent to beat was in good company.

Joe Carr wins the Amateur Championship

In 1953 he had reached the semi-final of the British Amateur Championship at Hoylake and only lost at the 19th to Joe Carr, who went on to beat the American holder Harvie Ward in the final by 2 holes. The Beamishes moved in early 1970, to Lincolnshire and Woodhall Spa but their two sons returned to Denham in the 1980s.

David Simons has been a member since 1958, when he captained the British Boys against Europe, and was one of the favourites to win the Boys Championship which was won by Braddon. He played twice for Cambridge in the University Match, once in the Dinner Match, and was captain of the Oxford and Cambridge Golfing Society in 1986–7. He appears in the record books for his experience at Muirfield when, playing against the Honourable Company, he had to suffer two opponents holing in one – in the morning at the 7th, in the afternoon at the 13th, both pitching into the hole full toss.

In the early post-war years the best player in the club was probably Hugh Browne and he was still good enough to win the Tarleton in 1956.

By then the playing resurgence was gathering momentum, helped by Nigel Hague, Dick Scott and John Tullis and soon by many other low handicapped players including Kingsley Borrett, later captain of the BB and O and in 1990 of Denham, Hamish Ritchie, captain of Oxford in 1965, John Uzielli, Michael Tilbury and, of course, Billy and Donald Steel.

Donald Steel was also a staunch and successful member of Gerrards Cross Cricket Club, as was John Trumper, and this became another source of new members. Tilbury, Trumper, Steel and Robert Farr all played cricket for Bucks, Tilbury making a hundred against Norfolk in his first match.

Another source of new members who were, or were to become, very good golfers can be traced to the election in 1968 of Geoffrey Brewer and of his wife soon after. Their small son, Ashley, had first struck a golf ball with cut-down clubs at Chorleywood and was old enough to join Denham in 1971. At Harrow he was a contemporary of A.A. Mann, Nick Tindall and Jamie Warman, all of whom followed him to Denham. Mann won the Tarleton in 1982, Tindall won the Club Championship once and Warman twice in the 1980s.

Jamie Warman went on to captain Cambridge and to be a consistent performer in the later stages of the President's Putter without winning it. The nearest he came was in the final of 1982 when he lost at the 19th to an eagle by Donald Steel, who thus won the Putter for the third time.

One of Jamie Warman's other achievements was a reversal of the normal father–to–son sequence of joining golf clubs. Mark Warman, who was shortly to retire as second master at Harrow, so enjoyed playing with his son at Denham that he and his wife dropped any other plans for retirement and came to live in Gerrards Cross, becoming greatly valued members of Denham. Thus it was that in 1979 the Pedagogues, a golfing society for schoolmasters, came to play the first match after its foundation at Denham, an occasion marked subsequently with the presentation by the Pedagogues of a fine bench, made by one of their number, which stands by the 1st tee in most weathers. One scarcely likes to tempt providence by mentioning that this match, played on the first Saturday in January had, after 14 years, not yet been stopped by the weather, though there was one year when, by 11 o'clock on the Saturday evening, a foot of snow covered the course.

Ashley Brewer brought the name of Denham Golf Club to the fore with a remarkable performance in the English Championship of 1982. This was played at Wentworth with the temperature in the upper 80s and even 90s throughout the week. With a handicap of 3 Brewer was lucky not to be balloted out but otherwise he needed very little luck in his progress through round after round until he reached the 36-hole final on the Saturday.

He was not done with yet, for after 16 holes he was 2 up on Craig Laurence and still 1 up at lunch. However, it had been an exhausting week for a genuine week-end golfer who, thinking that his participation in the championship would be only brief, had played in a 72-hole competition in

Hampshire on the Saturday and Sunday before it started. He had no answer when his young opponent, who at the time was expected to turn professional, played the 12 holes after lunch in four or five under fours.

For more than 20 years after the Second World War members of the US Air Force stationed at Ruislip were active temporary members of Denham. In the 1970s the US Navy, based in Grosvenor Square, became prominent. One of their number, Bob Nolf, was just about the best player at Denham and indeed won the Club Championship twice.

At the other end of the handicap scale, Wally Schwartz is a character remembered with much affection. On a sunny day Wally would look out of his office window in Grosvenor Square and, after a brief but one-sided wrestle with his conscience, would decide that he would serve Uncle Sam's cause better at Denham. As his service in the United Kingdom neared its end he must have been looking for a souvenir of Denham to take home, for in May 1974 he approached Nigel Hague, then captain, about a grandfather clock in the Artisan's club house. It was some time before the committee established the clock's working condition and possible selling price but in September this was done. Wally Schwartz arrived with a cheque for £25 and whisked the clock off on its long journey to Scottsdale, Arizona.

One of his colleagues, 'Lucky' Lucand liked Denham so much that after his retirement from the US Navy he stayed on and played almost every day, recording the result of every match in a notebook. He would tell you that he had won 173 golf balls and lost 137. If requested, he would reveal how you yourself had fared against him on previous meetings. Only when the lease of his house in Gerrards Cross ran out did he pack up and go home to Williamsburg, Virginia.

When their department was being split up and their golfers were either retiring or being posted elsewhere, the senior officer, Don Howard, made a charming speech of thanks for the hospitality which they had received and presented the club with the bell which hangs in the bar and is a highly effective means of procuring silence on a busy evening.

Among other overseas visitors in the 1970s was the Agent-General for New South Wales, Sir Davis Hughes, who when a minister in the New South Wales government had been closely involved with the building of the Sydney Opera House. He was a most sociable temporary member and made a lot of friends. The Agent-General for Victoria, Sir John Rossiter, was also made welcome but had to go home prematurely when his wife was taken seriously ill.

There is, of course, a long-standing reciprocal arrangement between Denham and the Woodlands Golf Club of Victoria. Occasionally a visiting member of Woodlands has been quietly absorbed into Denham. Woodlands is about an hour's drive out of Melbourne, well beyond the courses of the sand belt such as Royal Melbourne, Victoria and Metropolitan. The author of this book made his only visit to Woodlands on the Tuesday of the Melbourne Cup, a public holiday, and was overwhelmed by the welcome which he received from the captain, committee and senior members. These included two former cricket captains of Australia, Lindsay Hassett and Ian Johnson. Unfortunately the bush requires a straightness off the tee which he is seldom able to achieve for long and he failed to impress Woodlands members with the strength in depth of Denham golf. More recently, however, Kingsley Borrett's visits to Royal Cape with Robert Walker in 1990 and to Royal Johannesburg with Derek Graham in 1991 seem to have made a considerable impact on the two other overseas clubs with whom Denham has reciprocity.

In the early 1980s J.H. Atkinson was made an honorary life member on reaching the end of a spell of more than 20 years of sitting on committees since he followed Sir Roger Hollis as captain in 1957. His kindliness and concern for junior members led him for some years to attend the prize-giving after the Family Foursomes Competition, which was then open to husband and wife partnerships. If parent and child combinations were not among the prizes, Johnny Atkinson would himself slip in a prize for the one with the best score.

John Corbishley, a British Airways captain, was captain of Denham in 1966 and much missed when he retired to Lymington. Sir George Baker, president of the Family Division of the High Court, had a successful year of captaincy in 1967. Jack Moir was captain for the third time in the club's diamond jubilee year of 1970. As always, he was looking ahead and was considering how the 100th birthday of a lady member should be marked when the redoubtable Miss Kersey forestalled him by dying aged $98\frac{1}{2}$. He became president of the club in 1976.

Jack Moir was unlucky enough to suffer a severe attack of shingles affecting the face and his last few years before his death in 1983 must at the very least have been acutely uncomfortable. His had been the guiding hand which steered Denham through many of the hazards of the previous 40 years – he first became a director in 1944 – and it is often overlooked that at his best he had a single figure handicap, won the Tarleton twice, in 1947 and 1959, and the Rudd Salvers, with Pat Cotes-Preedy, in 1952.

Few captains can have had a more melancholy accession to the job than the vice-captain who took over in 1977 when Peter Dutton died half way through his year of office, but Sandy McIntosh handled matters with a sureness of touch appreciated by all.

Nearly every captain has cause to call on an architect for guidance on clubhouse maintenance or expansion. The mantle of Sir Giles Gilbert Scott eventually fell on Roger Royce, who became an invaluable adviser and a director. However, in the early 1980s he retired to Cornwall and went to live at Rock, a few yards from the St Enodoc clubhouse. Denham's loss was no doubt St Enodoc's gain and his death in 1991 will have saddened the members of both clubs.

In the early 1970s honorary membership of Denham was extended to four distinguished golf administrators on the grounds of their contribution to golf on a national and local level: Gerald Micklem, who as a player held the amateur course record of Denham for many years and as an administrator served every side of the game; Charles Lawrie, a leading golf course architect, non-playing captain of two Walker Cup teams and organiser of the Open Championship, who sadly died in 1976 aged 53; Myles Boddington, president of the BB and O; and Douglas Johns, secretary of the BB and O. Both Boddington and Johns went on to become presidents of the English Golf Union.

Their pleasure at what all four clearly considered a great honour was a source of considerable satisfaction to those responsible on the Denham side.

14 Alex Millar

FROM the 1960s running a golf club became a fight against heavy odds on several fronts. However well it was administered it could not escape the effects of deteriorating property and rising costs, but a greenkeeper of the calibre of Alex Millar was a great asset.

Denham's buildings, like those of many other sporting clubs, were reaching the age when they needed frequent maintenance and modernisation, perhaps expansion. No sooner is the kitchen brought up to date than the roof of the dining-room needs repair or the floor of the locker-room or the boiler or the bar. Not until you have to repair your property do you realise how much of it you have, both indoors and out. Fences have to be repaired, so does the drainage, the trees need lopping and so on. Modern machinery may be labour-saving but the initial outlay is considerable.

Surprisingly, the woodland at Denham suffered relatively little from the hurricanes of 1987 and 1989. A member living barely a mile away, with half an acre on a slope sheltered, one would have thought, from a south-westerly gale, lost six trees out of about 15. Even with only normal depreciation inflation presents problems undreamed of 30 years ago.

Between 1965 and 1992 the annual subscription for a full member will have risen from £20 to (including VAT) £658.

The individual benefactors who might once have been called on are, if not extinct, not to be expected. So there is no alternative to raising subscriptions and working out how much societies and green fee payers will pay – and still want to come. From early in the years of inflation the committee and directors seem to have realised the importance of keeping themselves informed not only about what clubs of similar standing were charging societies but also what they were paying their staff.

One of the Committee's best selections was made in 1966 when they appointed a new young head greenkeeper, Alex Millar, son of a Scottish professional and head greenkeeper. He and his brother had come down from Scotland a few years before. His brother became head greenkeeper at Moor Park and in the late 1980s Alex's son, young Alex, brought another course under the family's care when he became head greenkeeper at Stoke Poges.

Alex was assistant greenkeeper at Moor Park and playing for Hertfordshire against the BB and O when his opponent in the singles was Donald Steel. It was to lead to the start of a notable partnership. The traditional picture of a head greenkeeper being frustrated by an old fogey of a greens committee chairman who did not know much about golf, still less about the technical side of greenkeeping, did not apply at Denham, as for many years Donald Steel was chairman of the greens sub-committee or a member of it. He was impressed by Alex Millar's capacity for hard work. He recognised the problems of a greenkeeping staff and the need to keep the club equipped with modern machinery.

Denham may be one of the driest courses in winter but its gravel subsoil makes it one of the first to go brown in a hot dry summer. By August 1976 only 6 inches of rain had fallen at Denham in nearly nine months and though this was trebled by the end of the year, it was July 1978 before winter rules could be discarded.

In 1989 the course had another scorching and this time it was followed by a dry winter and another hot summer. Towards the end of the 1990 summer, however, the club bought an Arrifrance Micro 44 watering machine (cost £2,900) and though long rainless spells continued, the effect on the fairways was encouraging enough for a second machine to be bought for 1991. What with the cost of piping water in from the airfield and of building a machinery shed behind the club house, the total cost of the operation was not far short of £10,000 but in early July 1991 the fairways had made a miraculous recovery, winter rules were dropped and scarcely a bad lie was met. The course brushed aside a warm dry September.

After 25 years' service Alex Millar was made an honorary member. He remained one of the best players in Bucks at county level and it is easier to think of a competition he has not won than to list the number of similar tournaments in this part of the country which he has. He has won the national Artisans Championship five times.

Alex Millar

Donald Steel's contribution to the well-being of Denham Golf Club has been many-sided. No other individual member can have had more influence on the golf played at Denham than he did in the 1960s and 1970s whether re-siting bunkers; planting trees (no straightforward job in so well-drained a course); rebuilding the 10th green in the winter of his year of captaincy; putting into the fixture list the Christmas Fayre competition, designed to help the professional in case he had two barren months of snow ahead of him; and the creation in 1980 of a pitch and putt course out of a thicket.

A pupil of John Sheridan's from the age of eight, the young Steel was also active in the rugby and cricket seasons. It was said that other Scottish schools paled at the prospect of scrummaging against a Fettes second row of ten Bos and Steel. He was the first boy from a Scottish public school to be picked for the Public Schools at Lord's when he opened the innings in 1956. He was invited to play cricket for Cambridge – in the year of Ted Dexter's captaincy – but was not fit and never had another chance. He was captain of the Gerrards Cross Cricket Club.

His other commitments prevented him from playing in the Tarleton except in 1957 when he won it. His record remains played one, won one. His father had won it five years earlier. Donald won the Club Championship in 1969 and from 1971 to 1975. He did not enter in 1970 because it clashed with the Home Internationals and he was playing for England at Porthcawl.

At 19 Donald Steel was the youngest winner of the Tarleton and at 34 he was the youngest captain of the club when he took office in 1972. He shared, with Charles Lawrie, in a record unlikely to be broken, their 30 successive matches without defeat for Fettes in the Halford Hewitt.

At the same time he was golf correspondent of the *Sunday Telegraph* for the first 28 years of its existence, wrote frequently for *Country Life*, edited books including *The Bedside Book of Golf* and the massive *Shell International Encyclopedia of Golf*, and became one of the leading golf course architects of the day.

In 1981 another very fine player, Tony Parsons, formerly of Harewood Downs, joined Denham. A member of Shrewsbury's successful Halford Hewitt side and a formidable competitor, he won the Club Championship three times in the 1980s and the Tarleton three times in six years, this last a remarkable feat in an era when entries for the Tarleton Cup were exceeding 160. In the 36-hole final of 1991 he played the first nine holes in 32 and as able an opponent as Ashley Brewer was never able to recover.

A period of stability in the club house began when Jack and Joyce Lawton arrived as steward and stewardess in April 1970. A year later Brigadier R.E. Moss, previously at West Hill, came as secretary and he too stayed. Within a few months another highly regarded candidate for a secretary's job came to live in Gerrards Cross. John Leckie, while in business in Hong Kong, had run the cricket there and had greatly impressed visitors with his organising ability. It so happened that Gerrards Cross Golf Club also needed a secretary and he went there for seven years. Thus it was not until 18 months after Bob Moss's retirement that John Leckie took over at Denham – at a time of mourning for the death of the captain, Peter Dutton, whose last visit to Denham had been made to welcome him. Ten months later, in August 1978, John Leckie himself died suddenly while on holiday.

For some time thereafter Bob Fenning, recently retired from B.P. Chemicals, filled in such gaps as appeared in the succession until the arrival in 1984 of Wing Commander Derek Graham from Troon where his achievements had included involvement in staging the Open.

Jack Lawton had one memorable Sunday night during his years of stewardship. He was woken after midnight by a knocking on his door and found there a middle-aged man and a badly shaken woman. They had driven in through the gate on the 11th, which at that time was left open, and had parked on the left at the top of the hill which they had not noticed in the dark. Thus, when the car began to slide backwards down the hill at its steepest point, it came as a very nasty shock indeed. When it came to rest in the left-hand of the bunkers, they clambered out and went for help. They must have reasoned that in daylight even the most unobservant member would notice a car in a bunker and anyhow they now had no means of returning to their respective homes in North London.

Joyce Lawton made the woman a cup of tea. Jack got out his car and drove the couple back to the Finchley area, advising them to ring the secretary in the morning to recover the car and discuss compensation.

This was in Brigadier Moss's secretaryship and he clearly had a chance given to few to name any sum he liked, for the man would certainly have paid it, probably in cash. But, no doubt thinking that so reputable an establishment as Denham Golf Club should not stoop to anything smacking of blackmail, the brigadier settled for £15.

On the airfield side of the course there were mishaps of a more serious nature in the 1980s – three crashes by aircraft within five years and within about 30 yards of each other. In the first the pupil ran into difficulties while taking off and the instructor, aiming to land on the 18th fairway, just failed to clear the bunker at the top of the hill at the 9th. In the second accident the aircraft came down in the bushes just in front of the 4th tee and on the right. It caught fire and the pilot was killed. This was the only fatality in the three crashes.

Opening the pitch and putt course

The third occurred during an air display watched by a crowd of several hundred when a Blenheim, lovingly restored over several years and the only one still flying, came in, apparently intending to touch down and take off again. It did the first part of this manoeuvre adequately but, on being required to climb again, began to make ominous clanking noises. It went through the gap left by the previous accident, through the ladies' mercifully unoccupied 4th tee, bounced across the 9th fairway within a few feet of Maureen and Ian MacCaskill and came to a shuddering halt in the light rough between the 9th and 18th fairways almost on the spot where the first crash had ended.

15 An Illustrious Member

SOMEHOW this history has rambled on over events covering 80 years without mention of one of Denham's most famous members. Denis Charles Scott Compton CBE has been a member since 1957 and is part of the scenery. Only when you notice the eyes of visitors pop out as they see him, do you remember that for years he was one of the world's outstanding and most colourful cricketers, a batting genius, idol of many, and a good enough footballer to have won an FA Cup winner's medal for Arsenal in 1950.

Compton late cuts Bill Johnston to Archer at Adelaide. Benaud is an interested observer

In 1957, when he finished his professional career for Middlesex by making 143 and 48 at Lord's against Worcestershire, he had not long parted company with his right knee-cap, with which he had been in conflict for years as a result of a pre-war football injury. He was then 39 and was told that he could not expect to play any games after he was 55. He was in fact in his upper 60s when he played his last round of golf at Denham.

In the 1970s, when he had been writing for the *Sunday Express* for some 25 years, he found himself closely involved when the paper printed a scurrilous story. In effect this said that the toffee-nosed old fuddy-duddies of Denham Golf Club had snubbed and refused membership to Cilla Black and her husband, who had moved into The Grove, the house opposite the entrance to the course in Tilehouse Lane. This was not true. Mr and Mrs Bobby Willis had occasionally paid green fees and played a few holes but had not applied for membership. Such dealings as they had with the golf club had been perfectly friendly and indeed the Lawtons' daughter worked for them, looking after their children.

Denis was highly indignant, believing, with some justification, that people would think that he had prompted a piece which put Denham Golf Club in an unfavourable light. That Sunday evening, therefore, having consulted one or two other members without being discouraged, he stopped on his way home and knocked on Mr and Mrs Willis's front door.

At the sight of Compton they reached for a bottle of champagne. They were as embarrassed as everyone else, being afraid that they would be

Bill MacGregor, Ray Lindwall and Denis at Denham at the time of the 1980 Centenary Test. MacGregor, Australian by birth, worked at Hammersmith Hospital. Lindwall, was one of Australia's greatest fast bowlers, winning many Test matches for them during the post-Second World War period

thought responsible for the offending piece, but by the time Denis continued his journey home, goodwill abounded on all sides.

He must have been very nearly 55 when he became the joint-holder, with his opponent, of a record for stamina in the Tarleton. Until the 1990s the conditions of that competition laid down that if a match is all square after 18 holes, groups of three holes are played to settle the issue. One Sunday morning Compton and John Owen finished all square and started off again. They were still all square after 21 holes, after 24 and after 27.

They then agreed a short halt for half a pint of beer and a telephone call apiece to tell their doubtless incredulous wives, that they were going to be late for lunch and offering the feeble excuse that they were still playing their match. Operations were then resumed and they were all square after 30 holes. It was only on the 15th green, the 33rd, that Compton finally succumbed.

A recent compromise in the conditions of the competition almost certainly rules out this happening again. Now, after one group of three holes has been played, sudden death decides it.

Knowing how hospitable Australian golf clubs are to visiting cricket teams from England, Denis persuaded the committee, who did not need much urging, to offer the courtesy of the course to Australian touring teams. At that time Australian cricketers were not renowned for immaculate behaviour but their conduct at Denham was flawless and one could only hope that England touring sides in Australia were as appreciative of the hospitality which they received there.

16 Denham and the M25

FOR MANY years there had been speculation and apprehension about where the new motorway would go when the section through South Buckinghamshire came under consideration. It is only fair to say that anything which spared one driving, even once or twice a year, on the rolling twisting A 25 through Surrey, could not be wholly bad. Closer to home, it would be popular if it made the turning out of Tilehouse Lane into the North Orbital Road less of a problem. So the normal reaction to the new motorway was friendly – as long as it damaged someone else's property and not one's own.

Early in 1974 several possible routes for the South Bucks section were published and, when it was found that one went straight through the middle of Denham golf course, it concentrated the mind of members wonderfully.

The committee leapt into action and appointed a motorway sub-committee of three, led by Billy Steel, who became captain in April and devoted much of the first half of his year of office to the cause of saving the golf club. The others were Peter Dutton, a county councillor, and Scott Baker, a barrister – now The Hon. Sir Scott Baker QC, a High Court judge and captain in 1992. They attended numerous meetings and organised support from individuals and other bodies so that when in September they wrote an official six-page letter to the Secretary of State for the Environment, Denis Howell, it was not just the golf club which was protesting. Copies were sent to Ronald Bell MP, Bucks County Council, Beaconsfield District Council, Denham Parish Council, Colne Valley Regional Park, the Southern Sports Council, the BB and O, the English Golf Union and the PGA.

An appendix gave the club membership as: full male members 300, full lady members 100, junior, non-playing, country and overseas members 145, artisans (all resident locally) 40 and artisan juniors 8.

The letter pointed out that the club employed a staff of 13 plus about another 10 on a casual/part-time basis. The appendix setting out these figures also mentioned that part of the clubhouse dated from the 16th and 17th centuries.

The route being objected to was known as the Red/Yellow Alternative C. Going north, it entered the club's property from the railway, crossing the

11th fairway and running parallel to the 12th a few yards away from it. Having passed close behind the clubhouse, through where the staff cottages and the Artisans clubhouse stand, it swept on through the wood, emerging to knock off in quick succession the 18th tee, the 17th green, the 9th tee, the 8th green, the 4th green and the 5th tee. Only nine holes would have been unaffected, the four over the lane, the 6th and 7th and the 1st, 2nd and 3rd.

The sub-committee made sure that they could not be accused of dismissing lightly the possibility of replanning the course. They wrote:

> Having viewed the 6″ to 1 mile plans and longitudinal sections at one of the public exhibitions, a more detailed examination of the plans was undertaken at the South Eastern Road Construction Unit's Dorking offices . . . we have studied in detail the possibility of replanning the course within the present boundary to provide a total of 18 holes either side of the motorway by modifying existing holes and squeezing in extra holes. Unfortunately, it is not possible to produce an 18-hole course of a remotely acceptable standard. Even if it were possible, two bridges capable of carrying tractors would be required across the Motorway plus a road bridge for the southern access road from the Station to the Club House.
>
> We have also looked at the possibility of finding extra land adjacent to the golf course which might furnish us with the necessary extra holes. Such small parcels of land are sometimes produced in odd corners when a motorway is constructed. In our case, however, we are bounded by the airfield to the North, by existing housing to both the East and West and by the railway to the South. It is not, therefore, possible for us to find such extra land.
>
> The net result of this route is, therefore, to make it impossible for the Club to maintain an 18-hole golf course on the site.

The Sub-Committee had also had to consider Alternative Route D which would have passed close to the 10th green and would have crossed Tilehouse Lane a few yards down the hill from the entrance to the course, making the cottages there uninhabitable. The letter went on:

> This route would take some 1.7 acres of the Club's land [the other would have taken 19 acres out of a total of about 150.] and would encroach upon two staff houses. Even though relatively little of the Club's land would be taken by this route, it would have a seriously detrimental effect upon the course from the view-points of both noise and vision.

Having got the Minister up against the ropes, the letter slipped in two telling blows on one of his vulnerable parts – the cost of it all:

> We are satisfied, as explained, that if the Red/Yellow Alternative C were to be built, the continuation of Denham Golf Club on its present site would not be possible. The Club, therefore, would have to look for some 150 acres in the locality on which to build a new course and club house and we have grave doubts whether such a site with the necessary planning permission could be found. Even if it could be found, we estimate that, at 1974 prices and values, the cost of a new course of the same standard would be of the order of £1 million. This figure includes, *inter alia*, the purchase price of the land, the construction costs of an 18-hole course, a club house, five staff houses and outbuildings, together with professional fees and interest. It does not include consequential disturbance, loss of income etc.
>
> A further factor of importance with regard to the Red/Yellow Alternative C Route is

that in crossing the golf course it would necessarily have to cross a natural gas pipeline 24" in diameter, some 3ft to 4ft below the ground. We believe that this could be an expensive operation as the motorway would be in a cutting where it crosses the pipeline.

If no alternative site could be found and the Club had to close, it is clear that only a few of our members could be accommodated by other clubs in the locality. No monetary compensation could even begin to meet their loss nor, it would seem, is there any means of compensating the thousands of non-members who play at Denham every year.

The letter went on to point out that the closure would mean the loss of employment for the 13 permanent staff, some of whom had been with the club for many years, in particular the professional who had built up his business as a teacher and in his professional's shop for over 25 years. The pipeline carrying gas from the North Sea to the South Coast was a most useful supporting factor, for the mess made installing it was still evident where it entered the club's property by the 5th tee.

To make the point that it was not only the club members who would suffer if the course closed, the letter went on to give figures of the number of societies (74 in 1973) and of green fee visitors who would play in 1974. These totalled over 6,000, which was about 15 times the number of members who would play.

In the end, after a six-month public inquiry in Uxbridge, the Ministry came down in favour of the Green/Blue Route, as had always seemed likely.

Any intrusion into the life of a community is a guarantee of divisiveness. Gerrards Cross residents would have preferred Denham to have the motorway and vice versa. Some members of Denham Golf Club who lived on the eastern side of Gerrards Cross, within 200 yards of the Green/Blue Route, must have had the ultimate in mixed feelings.

On the other hand, as will be seen from the list of those to whom the letter was sent, some unusual bedfellows were acquired. It had cost the club a lot of money, effort and time to protect its interests but it had to be done and the club's leadership and the support which it received in the neighbourhood did it no harm at all locally.

17 The Course
by Bob Fenning

IT HAS already been recorded that the decision to construct the course was taken on 10 August 1910. The course was open for play on 29 May 1911. A very short time – at least by modern standards – and it does seem possible that some work was already in hand. Harry Colt was the architect and it is interesting that there is no record of any payment to Colt in 1910 or 1911. So it may have been that Major Way commissioned Harry Colt to start work early in 1910. The fact that his mother was made an honorary life member in 1911 shortly before her death gives some credence to this possibility.

At the 20th AGM in 1931, the retiring captain – who was our landlord, Lieut. Colonel B.I. Way – said that those who remember the course in 1911 'can hardly reconcile it with the course as it is today', so it is possible that play started while work was still going on. For all that, in 1913 for instance, the PGA Southern Qualifying Rounds were played at Denham and Fulwell. Of Denham it was said in *The Sportsman* that 'Everybody who attended that part of the Southern Qualifying Competition which took place at Denham came away impressed by the excellence of the course.' Of Fulwell it was said that the 12th hole, with its plateau green, caused much trouble. On this occasion, according to the paper '7's at this hole were as common as condemnations'. The writers in those days had a nice turn of phrase.

Denham Golf Club in those days was very different from what it is today, certainly in regard to the number of trees. Most of the trees between the 11th fairway and the railway were planted in the late 1950s by John Henderson in memory of his father. In the early days there were no trees on the right of the 2nd and 6th and the club was concerned about the danger to passers-by on Tilehouse Lane and Slade Oak Lane. Colonel Way presented the club with 2,000 trees in November 1913 and these were presumably planted in strategic places. Unfortunately there is no plan of the course in 1910–11 and it is not until 1921, when Colonel Reid presented the club with a plan of the course, that we have any idea of the layout.

The major differences concerned the 15th and 16th holes, the 15th being a dog-leg left, with the green somewhere near the present 16th green, and the 16th a short 120 yards across the road to somewhere near the present

17th tee. The plan in the colour section shows the layout and also the fact that the 13th back tee was an island tee, and the hole played over the quarry. There was no practice ground, and this was not constructed until after John Sheridan came.

During the First World War the course was obviously well looked after. In April 1921 a ladies open meeting was held and the *Morning Post* reported that 'Denham at this time of year is wholly delightful. It does not matter if you are there for stern business, in which case strings of 4's are your quarry, or whether a day in ideal surroundings, with such wild flowers as only Portrush could rival, satisfies you.'

There was of course no mechanisation at that time and it was horse and manpower that kept the course in trim. We employed upwards of 15 men on the course, and usually kept at least two horses. There were of course some hand mowers and indeed we lent – or gave – a mower to the local Army camp in 1915.

The upkeep of the tennis courts must have taken quite a large part of the work on the course. As will be seen from the plan there were two courts where the putting green is now, and two courts and clubhouse at the back. The tennis pavilion is now the clubhouse for Denham Artisans Golf Club. Tennis was played quite extensively before the First World War but never really got going again in 1919. There was some talk of making two hard courts at the bottom but the last mention of tennis was made in April 1922.

Over the years changes have been made to the course. Most of these have involved the removal and modification of bunkers and more recently the planting of still more trees. In April 1926 James Braid was invited to inspect

the course and make recommendations for alterations. In fact £1,500 was spent as a result of his proposals – the main one being that the 15th and 16th holes should be altered. This was in fact done and they became what they are today. Also he suggested that the first nine should be the second nine and vice versa, but that the 9th and 18th should be played as they were. This idea was in fact proposed by Mr McMeekin, a founder member, and the draft in the secretary's agenda book reads: 'That a trial be given to playing from the old 10th tee as tee No.1, continuing to the 17th and then playing from the 9th tee following on from the 1st old tee to the old 8th tee and then from the present 18th tee.' It obviously confused even the secretary! This was tried for some two months when it was unanimously agreed that the course should revert to being played as it was before.

Obviously the two wars had an effect on the course. During the First World War not only were trenches dug on the course in 1914, there were also local rules governing the trenches on the 2nd, 3rd, 4th, 6th, 15th and 18th. Why trenches should have been dug at Denham in 1914 is inexplicable but dug they were. Also 120 acres of land were earmarked for hay production in 1917 and, in April 1918, 500 sheep were allowed to graze on the course.

That the course was quickly returned to an 18 hole golf course there is no doubt and during the next few years some changes were made to the course, mainly in the placement and size of bunkers. For **instance, on 9 October** 1927 it was agreed that:

No.9 Hole – Braid's small pull Bunker – fill in old Turner Bunker – make good, highest point to be abutting on Fairway to be visible from Tee (Medal). Left new pull Bunker guarding Green – fill in inner third.

There is little doubt that all this was worthwhile, as A.C.M. Croome's 1926 eulogy of Denham Golf Club in the *Morning Post* confirms.

Denham is, I think, in Buckinghamshire. If it isn't, it ought to be, because it neighbours with Gerrards Cross, Chalfont St. Giles, Farnham Royal, and other picturesquely named beauty-spots. It can be reached in half-an-hour or so from Marylebone by a train which stops no fewer than four times within the tithing of Harrow. Harrow is a considerable place, containing a grammar school of some antiquity and repute. But a man passing through it on the way to his golf is tempted to think that its inhabitants are a bit pampered by the railway authorities.

It so happens that as the train draws into the

A.C.M. Croome

Denham Golf Club's Halt the passenger sees on his right the teeing-ground of the 11th hole and the first part of the fairway leading to it. This is bad luck, because it is the one bit of dull ground on the course. However, his apprehensions will be removed a minute later when he gets a glimpse of the putting-green, beautifully situated in a woodland dell at the foot of a steep slope. The approach-stroke played from the top of the hill to the green slightly raised on the further side of the dell and uncompromisingly guarded by cross-bunkers on the bank of it is almost unique, and promises a thrill.

Still looking down from the platform along the dell he will get a glimpse of the short 12th, an extraordinarily picturesque hole resembling in essential characteristics the Postage-Stamp at Troon, the seventh at Stoke Poges, and the eighth at Swinley Forest. The green is a shelf cut on the side of a steep hill, bunkered on the left so that you shall not bump the ball off the cushion to the pin, and ending in a sheer precipice on the right.

About the Bunkers

Until last week I had not been to Denham since 1912, shortly after the course was opened for play. But the smile of that dell had lingered with me all through the interval, and I beheld it again with joy and gladness, which a 4 and a 3 subsequently increased. My other recollections were less pleasant. I carried away from my first visit the impression that the busiest workers in Bucks were the worms and the bunker-makers. I take leave to think that some two score of otiose bunkers disfigure the landscape at Denham. But the worms have been utterly exorcised. Ground which fifteen years ago was fouled and soured by their casts is now singularly clean and covered by a rich and uniform growth of grass, on which the ball sits up inviting the addresses of the brassie – driver, if you like!

I do not expect to find universal approval of my doctrine that a golf architect should exercise the utmost economy in the cutting of bunkers; other prophets have been without honour in their own countries. But at least it will be granted that every bunker worthy of the name ought to do a decent job of work. I shall wager that at Denham there are far too many into which nobody ever goes, except a greenman with a rake, and occasionally a golfer so inefficient that it isn't worth while spending money on the provision and upkeep of artificial hazards for his entertainment.

At the same time it shall readily be granted that a rather liberal allowance of bunkers is required to 'make' the Denham holes. When the club acquired the property it consisted of a great plateau, or down, here and there boldly undulated, but otherwise lacking in natural features useful for the golf. Inevitably Art must supply what Nature has omitted. Having indicated that in my view the supply has been in excess of the demand, and being unable to find other cause for complaint, I proceed to describe the individual holes in greater or less detail.

The Clubhouse, a transmogrified farm, whose ancient barn makes one of the most beautiful luncheon rooms in the country, stands in the middle of the course, with nine holes on either side of it. This is convenient, because at week-ends the first teeing-ground can be reserved for properly-constituted matches; fourballers may be allowed precedence at the tenth.

Inspiring Start

We start the round with two specially good drive-and-iron holes. There is nothing very remarkable about the drives, but the first approach to a green some feet below the striker is interesting, and it makes some difference whether it is played from the proper place or not. Even more at the second, where the bunkers round the green are cunningly disposed, it pays to place the tee-shot.

The third is a very long two-shotter, and the second shot should be played from the left. Very properly there are some bunkers on the left of the fairway to introduce risk into the tee-shot. Those straight on the line, and at such a distance from the tee that anybody can carry them, should disappear. The fourth is also over 400 yards in length, but plays shorter than that, because the drive is downhill.

Then comes one of the gems, the fifth or 'Butts' hole, so called because it was here that the archers used to hold their wappenschaws before gunpowder was invented. It is a long short-hole played slightly uphill. The ground swings a trifle from the right, so that the bunker which blocks access from the left is not quite so terrible as it looks. One slips by it, and runs to the pin, or if one doesn't one looks forward eagerly to the next time of asking.

The sixth is played parallel to a sunken and out-of-bounds road overhung with trees, including Gospel Oak. The ground is canted to the left, and the green has been wisely built up so that it slopes, if anything, to the right. This is clever. The seventh is parallel to the sixth, and slightly longer, but reachable by the strong player in two good shots. The eighth is a beautiful short hole – a longish iron shot – with some very pretty runways before the green and a little stream waiting for a ball that drifts a trifle too much. To the ninth you drive uphill over an echelon of six bunkers, half of them mere eyesores. A strong player will just about get home with his second to the green by the Clubhouse.

Outward Score

The card says that the scratch score for the first nine holes is 38. That is a libel. Certainly the total length is close on 3,200 yards. But the putting-greens are so well contoured, their surface so good, the ground before them so trustworthy, and the lies through the green so uniformly easy that the good golfer, playing well, can be certain of getting the just reward of his every shot. The proper figure is more nearly 35, and personally I should not consider 34 unduly complimentary to constructor and greenkeeper.

The 10th is a good but plain hole of 400 yards, rather like the first, with a downhill finish. The two dell holes by the station I have mentioned. It's a bit of a climb to the 13th tee, and, having arrived there and recovered breath, you must play the deuce and all of a hole, most cleverly bunkered. You are subtly tempted to get as close as you can to the green in two, and, pressing to do so, you take six. The wise tactician will hit two safe spoon-shots and a longish pitch.

The fourteenth is a long two-shotter, and the fifteenth, played parallel to the sunken road and Gospel Oak, is like unto it, but is varied by the fact that its green is prettily terraced. The 16th is a short hole across a shallow dip in the ground. It is no disparagement to its quality to say that every course-architect keeps a sketch or plasticene model of such a hole in his work-room.

A Pretty Hole

The seventeenth is a thing of beauty, and would be more beautiful still if a bunker straight on the line of fire were removed. Its high bank prevents the player from seeing his ball well and truly struck from the tee leap forward to run down a pretty slope between the remains of an oak-forest on the right and a smaller coppice on the left to reach the bottom of the shallow ravine. Thence a nice high iron shot will place it on a wonderfully well constructed plateau green terminated on the left by a sheer bank leading to a patch of whins. The threat on the left often leads to disaster on the right.

The 18th hole is parallel to the ninth and forty yards shorter. Otherwise they are so much alike that a stranger might easily confuse t'other with which in reviewing his recollections of his first round at Denham. The inward half is shorter by some fifty yards than the outward. But the disposition of the length is such that there is no question between 35 and 34 for the scratch score. With the best will in the world I cannot make it lower than 35. That makes the total for the round 69, one or perhaps two strokes less than the proper total for the Old Course at St Andrews, where you find the essential conditions – *videlicet*, true, keen greens, trustworthy ground in front of them, and playable lies through the green – most palpably fulfilled.

In 1927 Harry Colt, the architect, was asked back to advise on the 10th and 16th holes, providing the cost was no more than £25. In 1933 he was asked what his fee would be for a plan of suggested improvements to the course. This was discussed by both the board and the club and in December 1933 it was agreed to go ahead with a number of changes – mainly to do with filling in bunkers. But tree planting on the right of the 2nd went ahead with both poplars and firs. In 1934, after a lot of discussion and indeed a ballot of members, Mr C.R. Fairey presented the club with the present shelter on the 1st tee.

In February 1935 there occurred a momentous decision. Dogs were to be allowed on the course but only as a trial!

Then came the Second World War and there were to be some significant changes to both the course and the clubhouse. A Home Guard tent was erected in the old bunker at the top of the slope on the 13th. The Air Ministry commandeered part of the course for the airfield and a fence was put in starting at the 2nd tee and finishing by the 4th green, thus putting out of play the 2nd, 3rd, 4th and 9th holes. The course was then played as follows:

War-time holes	Original holes used
1	1
2	10 (short)
3	11
4	12
5	13
6	14
7	15
8	16
9	17
10	4 from 9th tee
11	5
12	6
13	7
14	8
15	18
16	1 again
17	10 (short) again
18	Practice putting green (by clubhouse)

Holes out-of-use: 2nd, 3rd, part of 4th and 9th

Sam King driving at the 1st during a Red Cross Charity match in 1945. He is playing from the 'wrong' side of the Shelter because of war defences. Also playing were Arthur Lacey, a future Ryder Cup captain, Alf Padgham and Sandy Herd, both past Open champions

A group before the match: (left to right) *Turberville Smith, A.J. Miles, Major R. Way, Arthur Lacey, Mrs J. Hutchinson, Alf Padgham, Sam King, Sandy Herd and A.R. Shield*

After the war the course returned to its old format, but it is interesting to see that, in an Exhibition match with Alf Padgham played in 1945, Sam King is driving from the wrong side of the Hut. This switch of the first tee was due to the barbed wire that can be seen in the background.

Post-war – which period of time is more than half the life of the club – the changes were minimal. At first not much golf was played compared with today. The biggest change perhaps is that 30 years ago Saturday and Sunday mornings were quiet and the afternoons busy – John Sheridan remembers people queueing for tea on Sundays – now the pendulum has swung the other way.

The Course in about 1955

The 7th fairway

The 11th green

The Course in about 1955

The 12th hole

Panoramic view of course

18 The Sheridan Years
by Bob Fenning

THE PART that John Sheridan has played in the life of Denham Golf Club over the last 46 years is hard to exaggerate. Following the famous interview in London on Derby Day 1946, he first came to Denham by train and bus on the following Monday, Whit Monday, the day of the Victory Parade in London. He arrived at noon and was shown around the course by Major H.C.M. Stone, the captain. The course was still abbreviated as a result of the war and in the afternoon he played a round of golf with Major Stone, Jack Moir and Ken Hague and, as he says himself, he showed them every shot in the book! He then had tea with Pa and Reub Butler, and was then invited to come up on the Wednesday evening when the club was playing a match against the Artisans. He started with Denham Golf Club on the Saturday.

Pa and Reub Butler who both joined in 1939. In his later years Reub helped with club competitions and handicaps while Pa presented his trophy to be played for by the over 55s

John's first appointment had been as assistant to Angus MacDonald in 1936 at Swinley Forest. Things, as he says, were somewhat quiet! In 1937 Michael Bingham became the professional at Sunningdale and invited John to join him there. After serving with the Royal Artillery during the war he returned to Sunningdale and so it was from there that he joined Denham where he has been for the last 46 years. His father was caddiemaster at Sunningdale for 56 years, so long service certainly runs in the family!

When John came there was no practice ground – merely some land by the 4th and 9th tees and later on a small piece of land near the 3rd fairway. The 1st and 9th fairways were also used but no one was hit! But in 1955, largely at the instigation of

Dudley Cox, a member very fond of practising, the scrub land was cleared and the practice ground as we know it today was established. This meant that the 3rd hole, which had been a dogleg over the Himalayas was made a straight hole and the Himalayas removed. For the uninitiated, the Himalayas are the mounds on the left of the fairway and there was such an outcry that they were replaced the next year. In John's opinion the original hole was the best one on the course.

In John's early days he was responsible for the pin placing on medal and competition days and he and Charlie Stone, the head greenkeeper, would walk the course. As John says 'That was soon delegated'! Arthur Shields was secretary when John arrived but not for long and in the September the famous Harry Harrison arrived. John has a fund of stories of the man, but merely sums it up by saying that 'Harry had a great love of Denham.'

John was unmarried when he came to Denham and his accommodation above the shop was somewhat cramped. After he married Peggy, they moved to one of the Bailey Hill cottages before moving to their present house by the 13th tee.

Life was very quiet at Denham in the late 1940s – no societies – and a comparatively small membership especially in Denham Ladies Golf Club. Incidentally in 1939 there were 186 lady members of all categories. There were, as he says, very few good golfers in the club but that all changed largely due to the influence of Billy and Donald Steel. Societies started to be formed and to those societies that have been coming for a long time, John has become something of a legend. He always remembers them, and his computer-like brain always fits all of them and the members on the course with the minimum of fuss. But to the generations of Denham members he is above all a friend. A friend who has taught grandfathers and grandmothers, fathers and sons and mothers and daughters – and many more. He has taught them not only the basic principles of the golf swing but, perhaps more importantly, the etiquette of golf and how to behave on a golf course. When asked recently what Denham has meant to him he merely said 'It has been my life.' He is to very many members of other golf clubs, societies and to the members of Denham 'Sheridan of Denham'. It is therefore fitting that when he was rewarded with the BEM in the 1990 Birthday Honours List, Donald Steel should write the following in *Country Life*:

Salute to a True Stalwart

Reading through the Birthday Honours List requires a quiet hour and a sharp eye. It is easy to give up halfway through. Those who generally make the headlines inevitably get singled out, and when it comes to golf, they are usually Open champions. Tony Jacklin, Nick Faldo and Sandy Lyle have all been suitably honoured in the past.

Greater delight, however, can come from unexpected quarters. The simple

BUCKINGHAM PALACE

I congratulate you on the award
the British Empire Medal which you
have so well earned.

I send you my best wishes for your
future happiness.

Elizabeth R

John Charles Sheridan, Esq.,
B.E.M.

announcement last month that the British Empire Medal had been awarded to John Sheridan may have meant little to readers scanning the columns to the end. But to those who speak from first-hand experience of his 44 years as club professional at Denham, it said everything about his service to the game.

John Sheridan belongs to the band of unsung heroes whose influence is more permanent and far more widely felt than that of the outstanding players whose reward is measurable largely in terms of personal gain. He was of that generation of recruits who spent their entire time learning the skills of clubmaking and repairs, and maintaining the lengthy vigil necessary to keep and run a shop – only developing his own game out of hours.

At a time when there were only a few tournaments each year, Sheridan's appearances were limited to those in the London area. But in 1952 he established a record for the lowest score in the PGA's history for 18 consecutive holes. For years thereafter he had a bad round at Denham if he took more than 68. It was frequently 64 or 65.

He was appointed to his post on Derby Day 1946, making the short journey from Sunningdale, where he served his apprenticeship and where his father was the celebrated caddiemaster. For 56 years his father was friend and confidant of princes, figures in the world of entertainment and leading players.

Selfless Approach

Undoubtedly, the son inherited his father's sense of loyalty: an object lesson to professionals in every sport today, whose main concern is remuneration and a better contract. He also recognised from an early age that the welfare and enjoyment of members were of prime importance, and nobody has done more to live in accord with that doctrine.

At the root of his success in that regard has been the fact that he is a born organiser with a computer-like mind, adept at coping with the minutiae of competitions. Equally important has been the sergeant-major approach, ensuring that his directions are faithfully observed. Inherent in this are the sergeant-major's vocal accompaniment and his father's habit of saying whatever he felt needed to be said, whoever the recipient may happen to be.

But the characteristics that have made him stand apart are the help he has given to the young, and the no-nonsense way in which he has instilled into them the old-fashioned values of fair play, etiquette and good behaviour. He held junior classes long before it was fashionable to do so, conveying a simple message for which hundreds, young and old, have cause to be grateful.

It may be detectable by now that this is a personal salute. Sheridan's first days at Denham coincided with mine as a raw, plump, nine-year-old with only an elementary idea of how a ball should be hit. Whatever refinements have been added since are attributable solely to Sheridan. But I am not alone.

A unique aspect of golf is the respect and friendship that are established between members and their club professionals. As well as being worthy individual recognition of a lifetime's devotion, Sheridan's honour reflects the work of a battalion of club professionals. Some 90% of golf is played at club level, and it is these men who are the game's true stalwarts.

19 Handing On

A MAJOR object of this book was to provide present and future members of Denham with some record of the club's history before contacts are irretrievably severed by old age or the archives perhaps are lost or damaged. So the least one can do is to leave the author of a centenary book in the year 2010 with a picture of a club thriving, despite the economic pressures of the early 1990s.

Despite the cost of golf there is as yet no shortage of reputable younger members to maintain the standards. Even the High Court judges among the membership are young, or anyhow look young to a senior member. The ladies seem to become better players and better-looking all the time, not that there was ever cause for complaint in the past.

In November 1989 the club held a dinner unique in its history. Earlier in the month Hugh Bidwell, a member since 1973 and captain in 1980, had become Lord Mayor of London and had been knighted on taking office. At Sir Hugh's suggestion, a club dinner was held at the Mansion House and members were invited to bring their spouses and older children. For many it was a first experience of a City dinner and it was acclaimed with remarkable unanimity as a most enjoyable and memorable occasion.

In the first 80 years of its existence, Denham Golf Club has had only four professionals. For well over half this period the incumbent has been John Sheridan who, entering the 1990s, remained a much revered figure marvellously untouched by the passing years. When, in 1973, it was belatedly realised that nothing had been done to mark his first 25 years at the club, a dinner was given and two salvers were handed over to him as the prize for any competition he liked to name. He had always been keen for members to mingle rather than to play with the same group all the time, so he nominated a foursomes stableford competition open to men and lady members to be played on a Sunday at the beginning of the season, the draw for partners to be made on the Sunday morning. To accommodate as many members as possible it was to be a shotgun start.

In 1971 an early autumn fog had prevented play at the Autumn Meeting until 11 o'clock. The singles had to be postponed, the afternoon foursomes

were retained. To fill in time until lunch, Sheridan, who had long waited for
a chance to show that a simultaneous start would work, organised, with the
support of the captain, Colonel Robert Bridge, a nine-holes competition with
players starting at different holes. An earlier attempt to play the Spring or
Autumn meetings over two days, singles on one, foursomes on the next, had
not worked because many members were not available on both days.

With a growing number of entries for the Spring and Autumn meetings
the only way that the singles could be accommodated in one morning was by
a simultaneous start which allows 96 players to go off in three-ball matches,
one group at each of the four short holes, two at all the other holes.

This has its drawbacks, especially the congestion in the clubhouse as 96
players come in for a drink and lunch within a few minutes of each other.
But with Sheridan hustling players from bar to dining room and back again
and finding places for laggards with the energy of a skilled head waiter, the
foursomes get under way, if not punctually, at least early enough to avoid
fading light later.

One Sunday morning in the winter of 1990–91 the Lord Lieutenant of
Buckinghamshire came to Denham to read the citation and to present John
Sheridan with the British Empire Medal. No advance notice of the short
ceremony was given to members but somehow the word got round and more
than 60 gathered in the lounge to see the honouring of an old friend whom
Donald Steel has so felicitously called 'a true stalwart'.

Appendix

Captains

1912	J.C. Hibbert	1958	R.E. Allen
1913	W. Haldane Porter	1959	J.A. Henderson
1914–5	E.J. Sissons	1960	J.W.J. Moir
1916–20	E.Y. Dadley	1961	A.J. May
1921	C. Wyld	1962	J.M.T. Perry
1922–3	Hon. F.S. Jackson	1963	F.J. Trumper
1924	J.E.J. Burrows	1964	L.I. Baxter
1925	T.D. McMeekin	1965	F.D. James
1926	D. Cotes–Preedy KC	1966	J.A. Corbishley
1927–8	H.G. Muskett	1967	The Hon. Sir G. Baker OBE
1929	Sir G.G. Scott	1968	F.W. Barnes
1930	B.I. Way	1969	J.N. Woodbridge
1931	R.M. Rowley-Morris	1970	J.W.J. Moir
1932	G.H. Jennings	1971	Col. R.P. Bridge
1933–4	H.R. Rudd	1972	D.M.A Steel
1935	J.F. Tindal-Atkinson	1973	N.T. Hague
1936	W.G. Henderson	1974	W.J.A Steel
1937	C.T. Carr	1975	Dr J.C. Murphy-O'Connor
1938	G. Heron	1976	E.J. Yarrow
1939	C.R. Fairey	1977	P.A. Dutton
1940	A.F.I. Pickford	1978	A. McIntosh
1941–4	Turberville Smith	1979	R.I. Marshall
1945	R.B. Templeton	1980	H.C.P. Bidwell
1946	C.K.F. Hague	1981	M.C. Thomas
1947	Major H.C.M. Stone	1982	J.W. Gordon
1948	J.W.J. Moir	1983	J. Martin Ritchie
1949	Sir Giles Scott OM, RA	1984	D.E.F. Simons
1950	J.K.B. Dawson	1985	J.O. Trumper
1951	Myles L. Formby	1986	J.R.W. Walkinshaw
1952	H.H.R. Browne	1987	R.C. Vowels
1953	F.S. Harrison	1988	A.W.F. Clapperton
1954	W.B. Bryans	1989	R.D.R. Walker
1955	J.H. Butler	1990	J.G.K. Borrett
1956	R.H. Hollis CB	1991	P.H.P. Stephens
1957	J.H. Atkinson	1992	The Hon. Sir Scott Baker

Lady Captains

1912–3	Mrs Peel-Smith	1962	Mrs L.R.S. Cork
1914	Mrs Fea	1963	Mrs M.H. Lucking
1915–9	Mrs Forester	1964	Mrs Hartley-Clark
1920–3	Mrs G. Graham-Wright	1965	Mrs D.W. Moeran
1924	Mrs Hawkins	1966	Mrs F.J. Trumper
1925	Mrs Boyd	1967	Mrs J.A. Forbes
1926–7	Mrs Forester	1968	Mrs E.W. Braithwaite
1928	Mrs A. Gold	1969	Mrs J.M. Ritchie
1929	Mrs Bence-Trower	1970	Mrs P.R.G. Hembrow
1930	Mrs Burrows	1971	Mrs R.I. Marshall
1931–2	Mrs A.P. Saunders	1972	Mrs J. Cannon
1933	Miss Smyth	1973	Mrs A. McIntosh
1934	Mrs A.P. Saunders	1974	Mrs S.R. Elliot
1935	Mrs B. Morris	1975	Mrs P. McConnell
1936	Mrs Newton-Clare	1976	Mrs P.J.H. Hindley
1937–8	Mrs A.P. Saunders	1977	Mrs P.A. Dutton
1939–45	Mrs M.D. Purchase	1978	Mrs J.W. Gordon
1946–7	Mrs L.J. Whittaker	1979	Mrs F.M. Russell
1948–9	Mrs J.V. Daniel	1980	Mrs H.M.J. Ritchie
1950	Mrs G. Sutherland	1981	Mrs A.W.F. Clapperton
1951	Mrs K. Hague	1982	Mrs J.E. Woodward
1952	Mrs L.J. Williams	1983	Mrs I.W. Welsh
1953	Mrs H. Hartley-Clark	1984	Mrs M.C. Thomas
1954	Mrs C.W. Stothert	1985	Mrs P.H.P. Stephens
1955	Mrs F Trumper	1986	Mrs H.T. Easdale
1956	Mrs P. Rickards	1987	Mrs D.J.F. Dutton
1957	Mrs D. Walker	1988	Mrs W.H.M. Kirkwood
1958	Lady Hague	1989	Mrs R.N.D. Petter
1959	Mrs L.C. Hawkins	1990	Mrs J.O. Trumper
1960	Mrs J.V. Daniel	1991	Mrs H.J. Gibbins
1961	Mrs D.W. Moeran	1992	Mrs H.M. Lang

Secretaries

1911–18	Major W.E.S. Tyler	1975–7	Air Vice Marshal
1918–36	Major E.B. Hales		A.V.R. Johnstone
1936–9	Major R.S Boothby	1977–8	J.B.H. Leckie
1939–44	Major R.H. Way (Hon.)	1978–80	R.M.F. Fenning
1944–6	A.R. Shield	1980–1	K.M. Price
1946–62	F.S. Harrison (Hon.)	1981–3	F. Preston
1962–8	E. Radbone	1983–	Wing Commander
1968–71	A.N. West-Watson		D. Graham
1971–5	Brig. R.E. Moss		

Professionals

1910–14 J.H. Turner
1914–29 J. Rowlands

1929–46 A.J. Miles
1946–   J.C. Sheridan

Tarleton Cup

1912	E.J. Sissons	1956	H.H.R. Browne
1913	J.E.T. Burrows	1957	D.M.A. Steel
1914	G.E. Grant-Govan	1958	Myles L. Formby
1919	D.A. Rasbotham	1959	J.W.J. Moir
1920	J.S.B. Hill	1960	D.C. Grant
1921	R.M. Rowley Morris	1961	P.A. Dutton
1922–23	J.E.T. Burrows	1962–3	J.A. Corbishley
1924	E.G. Allen	1964	P.A. Dutton
1925	E.H. Cunningham Craig	1965	W.J. Uzielli
1926	G.H. Jennings	1966	J.G.K. Borrett
1927	E.A.S. Oldham	1967	J.A. Corbishley
1928	H.R. Rudd	1968	M.D. Dawson
1929	Sir G.G. Scott	1969	J.G.K. Borrett
1930	P.F. Walker	1970	O.J. Owen
1931	J.D. Kerr	1971	C.H. Beamish
1932	K.C. Holloway	1972	R.W. Krefting
1933	P.D. Cotes-Preedy	1973	R.D.R. Walker
1934	T. South	1974	R. Hatch
1935	E.J. Sissons	1975	A.W. Ritchie
1936	H.H.R. Browne	1976	M.C. Vowels
1937	R.B. Templeton	1977	J.L. Robson
1938	H.H.R. Browne	1978	A.P.S. Brewer
1939	H.C.M. Stone	1979	I.T. Leader
1944	H.C.M. Stone	1980	J.R.W. Walkinshaw
1945	D.C. Grant	1981	A.P.S. Brewer
1946	R.H. Hollis	1982	A.A. Mann
1947	J.W.J. Moir	1983	Dr J.C. Murphy-O'Connor
1948	A.R. Robson	1984	J.C. Payne
1949	D.C. Grant	1985	J.R.W. Walkinshaw
1950	R.S.G. Scott	1986–7	A.L. Parsons
1951	A.I.O. Davies	1988	J.G. Blyth
1952	W. Arkley Steel	1989	A.P.S. Brewer
1953	R.H. Hollis	1990	D.J. Knudsen
1954	R.S.G. Scott	1991	A.L. Parsons
1955	R.S.G. Scott		

Roger Way Challenge Cup

1949	Mr T.J. Barnes and Mrs T.J. Barnes	1972	Air Vice Marshal and Mrs C.H. Beamish
1950	Mr and Mrs R.S. Walker	1973	Mr N.T. Hague and Mrs A. McIntosh
1951	Mr F.S. Harrison and Miss M. Spier	1974	Mr M.C. Thomas and Mrs J.M. Ritchie
1952	Mr J. Tullis and Miss M. Spier	1975	Mr and Mrs D.J.F. Dutton
1953	Mr and Mrs N.B. Cork	1976	Capt R.S. Nolf and Mrs G.H. Roby
1954	Mr J.M.T. Perry and Miss R. Sherning	1977	Mr R. Hatch and Mrs F.M. Russell
1955	Mr R.S.G. Scott and Miss W.B. Bryans	1978	Mr R. Hatch and Mrs F.M. Russell
1956	Mr J. Tullis and Miss G. Rickards	1979	Mr J.C. Payne and Mrs N.E. Hampell
1957	Mr J.H. Butler and Miss A.K. Gibbs	1980	Mr and Mrs R.N.D. Petter
1958	Mr J. Tullis and Miss R. Sherning	1981	Mr O.J. Owen and Miss U.J. Melford
1959	Mr L.J. Baxter and Lady Hague	1982	Mr D.S. Ritchie and Mrs B. Reilly
1960	Mr C.H. Owen and Mrs R.A. Cork	1983	Mr A.L. Parsons and Miss N.A. Davies
1961	Colonel and Mrs F. Trumper	1984	Mr J.G. Blyth and Miss A. Walkinshaw
1962	Mr P.A. Dutton and Miss B. Trumper	1985	Mr D.W. Sayers and Miss P.L. Fergusson
1963	Mr W.J.A. Steel and Miss J.J. Drake	1986	Mr P.W. Ritchie and Miss E.M.N. Marshall
1964	Mr D.C.S. Compton and Mrs E.W. Braithwaite	1987	Mr J.G.K. Borrett and Mrs V.J. Irons
1965	Mr and Mrs P.A. Dutton	1988	Mr P.G. Vine and Miss E.M.N. Marshall
1966	Mr and Mrs R.I. Marshall	1989	Mr J.O. Trumper and Mrs H.M. Lang
1967	Mr and Mrs D.J.F. Dutton	1990	Sir Scott Baker and Mrs J. Gordon
1968	Mr and Mrs R.I. Marshall	1991	Mr A.G. Marshall and Mrs R.I. Marshall
1969	Mr and Mrs D.J.F. Dutton		
1970	Mr and Mrs P. McConnell		
1971	Mr J. McGrath and Miss R. Sherning		

Club Championship

1962	W.J.A. Steel	1978	J.M.T. Warman
1963	D.E.F. Simons	1979	A.I. Jackson
1964	W.J. Uzielli	1980	J.M.T. Warman
1965	R.V. Braddon	1981	A.L. Parsons
1966	D.E.F. Simons	1982	A.L. Parsons
1967	M.D. Dawson	1983	A.P.S. Brewer
1968	A.W.J. Holmes	1984	J.P.T. Stephens
1969	D.M.A. Steel	1985	J.R.W. Walkinshaw
1970	C.H. Beamish	1986	J.G. Blyth
1971	D.M.A. Steel	1987	A.L. Parsons
1972	D.M.A. Steel	1988	N.S. Tindall
1973	D.M.A. Steel	1989	J.M.T. Warman
1974	D.M.A. Steel	1990	J.R.W. Walkinshaw
1975	D.M.A. Steel	1991	A.L. Parsons
1976	D.S. Nolf	1992	D. Young
1977	D.S. Nolf		

The Max McDairmid Scratch Trophy

1971	Mrs E.W. Braithwaite	1982	Mrs H.M.J. Ritchie
1972	Mrs B. Dutton	1983	Mrs H.M. Fox
1973	Mrs E.W. Braithwaite	1984	Mrs R.I. Marshall
1974	Mrs J.W. Gordon	1985	Mrs H.M.J. Ritchie
1975	Mrs R.I. Marshall	1986	Mrs H.M. Fox
1976	Mrs R.I. Marshall	1987	Mrs H.M. Fox
1977	Mrs E.W. Braithwaite	1988	Mrs H.M.J. Ritchie
1978	Mrs H.M.J. Ritchie	1989	Miss E.N.M. Marshall
1979	Mrs B. Dutton	1990	Mrs H.M.J. Ritchie
1980	Mrs R.I. Marshall	1991	Mrs R.W. Lindsey
1981	Mrs R.I. Marshall	1992	Mrs F.M. Eckersley-Maslin

The Rudd Salvers

1934	D. Every Brown and T. South	1938	C.R. Chronander and W.H. Chill
1935	G.H. Jennings and Sir G.G. Scott	1939–44	No competition
1936	E.H. Titley and R.B. Templeton	1945	J.S. Lloyd and W.A. Steel
1937	B.W.T. Hare and M.J. Tyssen	1946	W.A. Steel and B. Butler
		1947	B.J.B. Sloley and A.R. Robson

1948	B.J.B. Sloley and A.R. Robson	1969	D.F.J. Dutton and C.N. MacKinnon
1949	H.F. Willmott and G. Emerson	1970	W.H. Kennedy and H.W. Try
1950	D.G. Grant and A.L. Wills	1971	M. Adamson and O.J. Owen
1951	C.R. Chronander and J.T. Barnes	1972	A.W. Ritchie and J.D. Bennett
1952	P.D. Cotes-Preedy and J.W.J. Moir	1973	R.M.F. Fenning and W.G. MacGregor
1953	F.J. Trumper and H.H.R. Browne	1974	W.J.A. Steel and W.G. MacDonald
1954	R.H. Hollis and R.S.G. Scott	1975	G.P.S. Brewer and J.E. Woodward
1955	G. Emerson and C.R. Chronander	1976	W.G. MacDonald and J.E. Woodward
1956	J. Corbishley and T.M. Bulloch	1977	R.W. Smith and D.R. Wynn-Williams
1957	J. Tullis and B.J.B. Sloley	1978	O.J. Owen and P. St. C. Proctor
1958	J. Tullis and B.J.B. Sloley	1979	R. Hatch and W.D.J. Crawford
1959	W.J.A. Steel and M.D. Dawson	1980	H.M.J. Ritchie and J. Sanders
1960	W.J.A. Steel and M.D. Dawson	1981	A.P.S. Brewer and G.P.S. Brewer
1961	W.J.A. Steel and M.D. Dawson	1982	A.L. Parsons and J.J. Butler
1962	P.A. Dutton and D.M.A. Steel	1983	J.A. Henderson and W.J.A. Steel
1963	W.J.A. Steel and M.D. Dawson	1984	G.P.S. Brewer and J.G.K. Borrett
1964	P.A. Dutton and D.M.A. Steel	1985	J.L. Robson and J.D.G. Buchanan
1965	H.H.R. Browne and J.R.B. Johnstone	1986	J.E .Dawes and A. Dawes
1966	W.J. Uzielli and C.N. MacKinnon	1987	J.E. Dawes and A. Dawes
1967	M.C. Emerson and O.J. Owen	1988	R.M. Hutchinson and J.N. Davie
1968	H.M.J. Ritchie and P.J. Hembrow	1989	A.D. McCallum and J.W. Attwood
		1990	D.R. Beamish and M.F. Beamish
		1991	P. Sedgwick and O.J. Owen